'MANTLE OF THE EXPERT' THROUGH SHAKESPEARE

Dorothy Heathcote Guides Life
Learning for Motor Vehicle Mechanics,
Takes Shakespeare Workshops and
Inspires Music for Special Needs Pupils

WENDY JEAN MACPHEE

SINGULAR PUBLISHING

'Mantle of the Expert' Through Shakespeare
Singular Publishing, Norwich, UK

© Wendy Jean Macphee 2021

All rights reserved. No part of this book may be reproduced, stored in a retrieval system or transmitted in any form or by any means, electronic, mechanical, photocopying or otherwise, without the prior permission of the publisher and copyright owners

The right of Wendy Jean Macphee to be identified as the author of this work has been asserted

This book is sold subject to the condition that it shall not, by way of trade or otherwise, be lent, resold, hired out or otherwise circulated without the publisher's prior consent in any form of binding or cover other than that in which it is published and without a similar condition being imposed on the subsequent purchaser

A CIP record for this book is available from the British Library

ISBN 978-1-8381283-4-0

www.singularpublishing.com

IN MEMORY OF
DOROTHY HEATHCOTE

AND FOR MARIANNE, KEVIN
AND ANNA HEATHCOTE WOODBRIDGE

CONTENTS

Preface

CHAPTER ONE—THE BEGINNINGS

    The Challenge   13

    Aspects of the learning stratagems of Dorothy Heathcote's 'Mantle of the Expert' drama-in-education principles applied in this work   16

    Additional factors that were necessary to make the dramas acceptable to most of the students   21

    The nature of the classes which were involved in the filmed dramas   24

CHAPTER TWO—*TWELFTH NIGHT* (ACADEMIC YEAR 1978–79)

    Themes of the play *Twelfth Night* analysed in terms of their universal application to everyday life   29

    Filming with class MVM 1E   32

    Filming with class MVM 1C   38

    Filming with class MVM 1A   45

CHAPTER THREE—*AS YOU LIKE IT* (ACADEMIC YEAR 1979–80): CLASS MVM 1E

    Themes of the play *As You Like It* analysed in terms of their universal application to everyday life   51

    Class MVM 1E   54

CHAPTER FOUR—*AS YOU LIKE IT*: CLASSES MCC 2A AND MVM 3C

    Class MCC 2A   61

    Class MVM 3C   67

CHAPTER FIVE—*AS YOU LIKE IT*: CLASS MVM 2D

    Class MVM 2D   73

CHAPTER SIX—*THE TEMPEST* (ACADEMIC YEAR 1981–82);
SUMMERFIELD CENTRE (2000–01); REFLECTIONS

   The Tempest   85

   Summerfield Centre   86

   Reflections on the work with mechanics students
   and young people excluded from school   88

CHAPTER SEVEN—SPIN-OFF; ORAL WORK WITH SECRETARIAL
STUDENTS (ACADEMIC YEARS 1978–80); CONCLUSIONS

   Spin-off   94

   Twelfth Night and *As You Like It* used as a source of oral
   teaching material for secretarial students in the Southgate
   Technical College Business Studies Department   97

   Conclusions   99

CHAPTER EIGHT—THE WORKSHOPS OF *ANTONY AND CLEOPATRA*
AND *MUCH ADO ABOUT NOTHING* THAT DOROTHY HEATHCOTE TOOK
WITH STUDENTS OF THE MENCAP NATIONAL COLLEGE, DILSTON,
NORTHUMBERLAND

   Antony and Cleopatra (1998)   101

   Much Ado About Nothing (1999)   104

CHAPTER NINE—SOME OF DOROTHY HEATHCOTE'S LIFE-LEARNING
STRATAGEMS APPLIED TO ABLE-BODIED CHILDREN AND TO THOSE
WITH SPECIAL NEEDS

   Music for special needs pupils (1998–2003)   110

   Other special needs subjects (1998–2003)   116

   The use of 'secondary role' in private tutoring
   of pupils in English language and literature   118

CHAPTER TEN—CONCLUSIONS   121

   Notes   125

   Biographies   128

LIST OF ILLUSTRATIONS

Moments performed by Theatre Set-Up in the plays *Twelfth Night* (1979) and *As you Like It* (1980) which correspond with the themes given to the students.

Fig. 1 *Self-indulgent Emotion*, Orsino's suit of Olivia (*Twelfth Night*, II. iv.) Forty Hall
Fig. 2 *The Person who is Ambitious*, Maria (*Twelfth Night*, II. iii.) Forty Hall
Fig. 3 *Deceit*, Viola in Disguise (*Twelfth Night*, I. v.) Forty Hall
Fig. 4 *The Conman and the Dupe*, Sir Toby Belch and Sir Andrew Aguecheek (*Twelfth Night*, II. iii.) Forty Hall
Fig. 5 *The Outsider*, Malvolio and Sir Toby Belch (*Twelfth Night*, III. iv.) inside Forty Hall
Fig. 6 *Relationships within a Firm*, The Fool and Malvolio (*Twelfth Night*, II. v.) Forty Hall
Fig. 7 *The Brothers*, Orlando protests to Old Adam about his brother's mistreatment of him (*As You Like It*, I. i.) Forty Hall
Fig. 8 *The Boasting Boxer*, Charles the Wrestler (*As You Like It*, I. ii.) Chaplaincy Gardens, Isles of Scilly
Fig. 9 *Prejudice,* (losing the respect of his own family) Duke Frederick against Rosalind and Orlando. His daughter, Celia, leaves her father and pledges to accompany Rosalind into exile (*As You Like It*, I. ii.) Forty Hall
Fig. 10 *Disguise*, Rosalind (*As You Like It*, IV. i.) Tresco Abbey Gardens, Isles of Scilly
Fig. 11 *The Flash Guy and the Steady*, Touchstone courts Audrey (*As You Like It*, III. iii.) Forty Hall
Fig. 12 *The Flash Guy and the Steady*, Touchstone and William court Audrey (*As You Like It*, V. i.) Tresco Abbey Gardens
Fig. 13 *The Ideal Society*, In the Forest of Arden (*As You Like It*, II. vii.) Lyme Hall
Fig. 14 *Disguise,* Rosalind with Orlando and Celia (*As You Like It*, III. iii.) Forty Hall

PREFACE

This volume aims to promote the guidance and inspiration of the educational luminary Dorothy Heathcote to my teaching from 1978 to 2012.[1] The necessity to document her contribution to my time spent in schools, colleges and private teaching is urgent as some aspects of her 'Mantle of the Expert' system which we discussed and practised together have not been mentioned or emphasised in other publications. In 1977–78 I used a year's sabbatical leave to take the Drama-in-Education course at the University of Newcastle-upon-Tyne. I was privileged that the lecturer of the courses at this university and the consequent source of the variety of drama-in-education projects which are discussed in this book was Dorothy Heathcote. This culminated in a Diploma in Drama-in-Education in 1978 and a M.Ed. by thesis degree (which I studied part-time) in 1981.

I have demonstrated in this text that aspects of Dorothy Heathcote's teaching mantras have had a continuous historic recorded source as far back as ancient Rome. I adapted them by: using themes from Shakespeare's plays in order to promote life-learning for motor vehicle mechanics and oral work for secretarial students; making performances of those plays accessible for the motor vehicle mechanics through the life-learning sessions; participating in Dorothy's workshops with Mencap students on *Antony and Cleopatra* and *Much Ado About Nothing*; examining universals as the proper content of any school or college syllabus through comparing the universals in the Shakespeare themes with those suggested by Georges Polti in his *The Thirty-Six Dramatic Situations*;[2] using inanimate objects in secondary role in all subjects, particularly music for young people, especially those with special needs; and always using objects to represent abstract concepts for pupils and to make stories, songs, and dramas real with props, costume and suggested scenery.

My teaching and academic life began in South Australia, gaining at Adelaide University, in addition to teaching qualifications, the B.A. degree in 1960, and the diplomas, Licentiate of Speech and Drama of Australia in 1962 and Associate of Music of Australia in 1959. After teaching in Adelaide for three years, in 1963 I travelled to the UK to pursue further theatre studies, teaching in schools in London and qualifying for the Licentiate of the Royal College of Music in Speech and Drama Teaching in 1968 through studying part-time at the Central School of Speech and Drama. From 1968 to early 1969 I was a drama tutor in the professional acting course faculty of Manchester College of Art. In 1969 I returned to London to become a lecturer (initially in Drama, English and Liberal Studies and from 1982 onwards in GCSE and A level Theatre Studies) at Southgate College until 1991. From 1982 to 1996 I was diverted from 'Mantle of the Expert' teaching in studying Arcana in Shakespeare at the Shakespeare Institute of the University of Birmingham for my Ph.D. (1996) and teaching GCSE and A level Theatre Studies at Southgate College (in a 'road map' style of teaching as Dorothy called it – see p.16).

The first of these projects (at Southgate Technical college as it was then called) I recorded in diary form as part of my Master of Education degree which was supervised by Dorothy. These consisted of sessions with a variety of students, but mainly with motor vehicle mechanic apprentices, in filmed drama-in-education programmes. These aimed to make accessible to them several Shakespearean productions presented by the professional theatre company Theatre Set-Up, which I ran during the college summer vacation.[3] Dorothy suggested that I combine my work at the college with that of the theatre company. Themes from Shakespeare's plays were also used to train secretarial students in their business oral work. Throughout most of these drama-in-education enterprises the significance of the universality of the themes in Shakespeare's plays and their importance as a source of material for school and college curricula became evident. The main content of the sessions aimed at life-learning and evolved from the themes which benefited the students according to their needs.

The demand for Theatre Set-Up's productions grew over the years from its inception in 1976 and its inclusion in the Southgate

College drama-in-education sessions so that it served heritage venues throughout the UK for 35 years and ultimately in mainland Europe for 19 years. It was a registered charity, employing professional actors and costumiers, and observing the British Actors' Equity terms and conditions for its employees. The company proved of considerable benefit to students at Southgate College – not only to the work with the vocational students in 1978–81, but to my Theatre Studies students from 1982 onwards. My theatre skills were honed by mounting and taking part in the productions during the college summer vacations and any of the Southgate Theatre Studies students who had the potential to be professional actors or theatre technicians had the possibility of access into the company after they had received training at one of the major UK Drama schools. Another benefit to my Southgate students was supplied by my professional theatre associates. Any students' project work on aspects of theatre which were required by the Theatre Studies syllabus was welcomed by my colleagues in associated theatre companies who gave my students access to good professional material for their submissions to the examining board. Thus the combination of the work of the college students with that of the Theatre Set-Up company which Dorothy had initiated in 1978 proved to have lasting advantages both to the students and to Theatre Set-Up who benefited from the excellent services of the Southgate alumni. In 1998 and 1999 Dorothy, who had by then become a trustee of Theatre Set-Up, joined forces with the company again, running workshop sessions for the students of Dilston Mencap College introducing them to the company's performances of *Antony and Cleopatra* and *Much Ado About Nothing* (which were held in the college grounds).[4]

Retired from full-time work, in 1998 I began to do relief teaching in a wide range of schools, including those providing for special needs and pupils excluded from school, where Dorothy's drama-in-education 'Mantle of the Expert' principles, applied to a range of subjects especially music, proved beneficial.

I found that the most remarkable of all these drama-in-education projects was that inspired by Dorothy's amazing guidance on the life-learning evolved from the work with the Southgate Technical College mechanics students in making Shakespeare accessible to them. Unfortunately the films and tapes which recorded the work done by them became corrupted over the years and had to be thrown away, but the diaries record the work exactly as it was done. The students considered the work that was done to be strictly private. Respecting this, only first names are used of both staff and students in the following account of the sessions.

It is important to note that the sense in which the 'Mantle of the Expert' is used herein is not the same as that applied to work with school children – a threefold process involving the features of 'expert', 'client' and 'commission', which Dorothy Heathcote developed in the 1980s and which is recorded in her and Gavin Bolton's book *Drama for Learning* and Tim Taylor's book *A Beginner's Guide to Mantle of the Expert* – but rather just the application of the 'expert' feature, endowing the students/pupils with its qualities.[5] The features of 'client' and 'commission' were developed after I did my work with students in 1978–81 and they were mostly applicable to work with young pupils. They were not relevant to the later teaching I was doing with subjects such as English tutoring and music with special needs pupils.

I would like to say that in my long teaching career, I found the work that was inspired by Dorothy the most exciting and satisfying. The students involved in this kind of life-learning were engaged, responsive, creative, and often thrilled by the effects of the dramas which they learned by being given self-determined pleasurable experiences. I hope to share that excitement and satisfaction with other teachers and practitioners.

Dorothy Heathcote

Fig. 1 *Self-indulgent Emotion*, Orsino's suit of Olivia (*Twelfth Night*, II. iv.) Forty Hall

CHAPTER ONE

The beginnings

THE CHALLENGE

My teaching life that was guided and influenced by Dorothy Heathcote started as an adventurous experiment. The story of this experiment in applying Dorothy Heathcote's principles of drama-in-education to community life-learning was begun in 1978 at what was then called Southgate Technical College in North London.[1] This was a very exciting Further Education establishment whose students represented all parts of the community and whose lectures covered many fields. There were seven major departments: Business Studies, Catering, Educational Technology, Electrical Engineering and Science, Fashion and Distribution, Mechanical Engineering, and English and Liberal studies which included A level arts and science subjects (including music and drama), with part and full-time day classes. In order to give people who worked during the day the chance to further both their occupational skills and general educational interests, evening sessions which included many subjects such as opera, orchestra and theatre, opened the college to anyone who wanted to enjoy what it had to offer. All the classrooms in the college were fully occupied from 9am to 9pm during weekdays and such was the demand for the courses of the college that in 1976 an additional floor had to be added on top of the main building and a large library was built on one half of the gardens in the front of the grounds.[2]

As a drama lecturer putting on productions of plays in the College Theatre and Octagon Studio I found this mix of people a rich source of talent and expertise and the young day-time students enjoyed the participation of the evening class adults in their plays. It was always a challenge to involve day-time craft practice students in productions of plays. We succeeded in doing this when we presented the *Prometheus Bound* of Aeschylus and the *Iphigenia in Aulis* of Euripides in the Octagon Studio, with senior Greek Cypriot full-time motor vehicle mechanic students playing some of the male Greek characters in the productions, giving the plays a genuine ethnic reality with the young Greeks' physical and emotional vigour. When these young people made their entrances to the plays, the audience felt the rolling back of two and a half thousand years as the ancient dramas achieved a modern relevance.

However the challenge still remained of inspiring day-time release craft practice students such as motor vehicle mechanic apprentices to participate in or to enjoy any theatre or art that they considered to be outside the accepted bounds of their 'working-class culture'. The problem was presented to me by the Vice Principal of the college during my interview for appointment to the lecturing staff in English, Drama and Liberal Studies in 1969. When I expressed an interest in trying to involve the motor vehicle mechanic students that I would be teaching in performing and viewing dramas, he said that it would be impossible; that they had never expressed an interest in drama, never went to see plays and resisted all attempts to be enticed to see them or be involved in any 'cultural' activities (which they considered to be effeminate).

A year's sabbatical leave from 1977–78, studying the Diploma in Drama-in-Education course at the University of Newcastle-upon-Tyne with Dorothy Heathcote offered a solution to that problem. On this course we studied the application of Dorothy's principles of drama-in-education, most of which she called 'Mantle of the Expert', which means that the pupils put on the 'mantle', symbolising the professional attributes and status, of the experts in the field which is the subject of their drama, thus gaining control and responsibility. Dorothy herself is quoted as saying, "The mantle means I declare my calling and live up to what is expected of me in the community ... I use it as a quality of leadership, carrying standards of behaviour, morality, responsibility, ethics and the spiritual basis of all action."[3] The sessions in Dorothy's University of Newcastle-upon-Tyne course were also conducted outside the university with many different kinds of groups of all ages: including residents of the homes for mentally disabled adults and children which were then in existence, and with infant, primary and secondary school students.[4]

She showed us films which had been taken of her working with many different groups from all over the world in sessions which she had been engaged to give in those countries. Whatever the nature of the 'pupils', whether adults needing instruction in an aspect of their work, or children needing to acquire life-learning skills or to have experience of difficult aspects of their school syllabus, her methods succeeded in achieving the aims of the learning.

She emphasised to our class the need not to rush the process of the dramas but to listen to the needs of the pupils and move the drama accordingly. This, she claimed was her reason for our doing so much work with people who were learning disabled as they needed the time to absorb and react to the dramas. Often she used the framework of legendary stories such as children's fairy tales with younger pupils. She gave the class I was in an example of this in a workshop in one institution with a group of sessions centred on the fairy story of the prince who had been turned into a frog. Among many things, this drama taught the power of love. I was lucky to be able to use what I had learnt from all this work in later years when working in special needs schools in Essex and North London.

In 1978 when I returned to my job at Southgate Technical College from my year's sabbatical leave course with Dorothy Heathcote, I was given, along with my usual day-time and evening class drama students, many motor vehicle mechanic apprentice classes who were to take the English and Liberal Studies courses. The University of Newcastle-upon-Tyne had suggested to me that I might like to continue working with Dorothy on a part-time Master of Education course. By then, Theatre Set-Up, the theatre company I had started in 1976 which performed Shakespearean plays in the gardens of its home base of Forty Hall, Enfield, had become professional in order to tour Shakespearean plays to National Trust venues that were eager to have them. The play to be performed by the company in 1979 was *Twelfth Night* and in 1980 *As You Like It*. Dorothy and I decided that we would try to make these plays accessible to the motor vehicle mechanic apprentices and any other of the pupils I was to teach at the college, using whatever principles of her 'Mantle of the Expert' method of life-learning should prove relevant and applicable. We thus embarked on an exciting two years' experiment involving all of my Southgate Technical College pupils, using the excellent facility of the small college television studio and any other equipment that our very competent technical staff could provide.[5]

ASPECTS OF THE LEARNING STRATAGEMS OF DOROTHY HEATHCOTE'S 'MANTLE OF THE EXPERT' DRAMA-IN-EDUCATION PRINCIPLES APPLIED IN THIS WORK

Examples of how these were practised in the educational dramas with the Southgate College students or in other projects featuring Dorothy's work, are enclosed in brackets. N.B. It is important to note that Dorothy also said that this method of creating learning is not always appropriate: "Sometimes you just need a road map."

1 – **The unknown material to be learnt is presented in the form of a metaphor which links it to the known experience of the students.** (The selected metaphor for the *As You Like It* 'Golden World' pastoral location of the Duke Senior and his followers in The Forest of Arden was presented as 'An Ideal Society' in class MVM 2D p.77.)

2 – **This metaphor is acted out by the students in the dramatic form whose events are suggested by them, the member of staff functioning as a 'teacher facilitator', drawing out any areas of learning that might result from the dramas. All courses in the actions of the story and decisions taken in the dramas must be made by the students. This is the sense in which they put on the 'Mantle of the Expert'.** (I learnt to allow the students to have free rein in the dramas when Dorothy once said to me, "Put your ideas away in a drawer, Wendy." The effectiveness of the kind of 'Mantle of the Expert' role appropriate to this kind of drama-in-education is

demonstrated in a film of Dorothy's work with very young pupils in a programme in the United States whose imagined setting was on a farm where land was being divided up among the pupil 'prospective farmers'. She was in role as one of the 'prospective farmers' and at one point pretended in role to fall asleep when the pupils were in role as 'the experts', legislators taking decisions about land distribution. She then pretended to wake up and protest that she had not been given enough land even "to grow a carrot or run a chicken". The pupils looked suitably abashed and life-learning took place for them about the need to consider the welfare of other people when making decisions).

3– **Respect is given to whatever the pupils/students say, whatever that may be. If they make suggestions for the drama to be performed which might seem to be 'showing off', asking for unreasonable conditions or ridiculing the dramatic process, the teacher treats those suggestions seriously and examines the possibility of responding to them positively.** (When a member of class MVM 1E (p.32) shouted out, "Can we have girls in our story?" I replied "I will ask some girls if they would like to join you but you must treat them with respect." Several girls agreed to do this and I subsequently learnt that they had an influence over the boys that far exceeded my ability to promote learning in the drama. When another class asked for a girl "with big tits" to join them, a drama student with that qualification agreed to act with them. They were astonished at my compliance with their rude request. Modestly unaware of the reason she had been chosen to perform in that class, she took her role in their story so seriously, that the boys forgot about her physique, and she engaged them with her integrity within the drama to such an extent that she had them 'in the palm of her hand' throughout the sessions as she promoted the needed learning exposed by the stories. This outcome justified, at least in this instance, the principle of taking the student's rude comment seriously.)

4 – People are often brought in to act specific roles which promote the learning. These 'actors' have been briefed with the learning aims of the drama and attitudes that they might adapt within the drama in order to draw out the learning objectives. Sometimes inanimate objects can be used in what Dorothy called "secondary role". (In many of the classes girls from the A level drama class which I taught acted in role. In class MVM 1C in 1978–79 and in class MVM 1E in 1979–80 members of staff acted in role and in class MVM 2D in 1979–80 a visiting drama-teaching student. If the drama is not succeeding in creating learning, sometimes it is necessary, if that is possible, to bring in other people in additional roles. The only roles it was appropriate for me to take in order to allow the students their freedom in taking decisions and suggesting ideas for the dramas were those monitoring the outcomes or creating order, such as that of the chairperson of a tribunal in 'The Ideal Society'. Sometimes if the student acting a role in the drama was absent during the filming of an episode I would take that role, making sure that I did not impose my own decisions on the story. During the workshops at Dilston College on making the *Antony and Cleopatra* and *Much Ado About Nothing* performances being presented there by Theatre Set-Up accessible to the students, Dorothy in addition to her main role as 'guide' on the journey through the play, adopted many roles monitoring the learning and creating a sense of the scene, plot and characters, such as holding out her hands to become the outer frame of the Roman ship, encouraging all the students to do the same. As the 'guide', in fact in teacher facilitator role, she asked questions of the actors – in role in their costumes – which clarified the characters' motivations and dramatic intentions. For example, she asked the actor in role as Enobarbus why he had deserted Antony.)

5 – **In order for the learning of the drama to be successful, the teacher takes continual steps to 'deepen belief' in the story and its characters.** (Often, just referring to details within the imagined scenario can 'deepen belief'. In the film *Three Looms Waiting*, available on the internet, Dorothy has accepted the class suggestion that their drama should be set

in a prison camp: "Show me your guns!" she sharply said to the pupils, immediately deepening their belief in their imagined setting as they mimed rifle-type guns of prison guards.[6] In using an additional person in role to deepen belief with the *As You Like It* class MVM 2D drama of 'The Ideal Society', I suggested, in role as the chair of the tribunal (see p.79), to the pupil acting the part of a husband who did not want his 'wife' (the class had decided not to have formal marriage) to have an abortion, that his 'wife' should take part in the tribunal's decision and that we should bring her in for the next filming session. His eyes lit up and he said, "Can we bring in my wife?" This would be a role-playing visiting drama-teaching student whom he totally accepted as his 'wife' within the story when she entered the next session. When, during the filming, the tribunal suggested that if the community's nursery could look after the new baby, he should look after their three-year-old, again his eyes lit up with pleasure and he said, within role (seemingly unaware that this was a created story, a characteristic of good professional actors) that he would like to do that. The bringing in of a person in role as the 'wife' at the heart of the drama deepened the belief in the story for the pupil in role as the husband.)

6 – **The learning that emerges from the dramas being performed by the students can ultimately relate to the original aim of the process, but the 'teacher facilitator' needs to be alert to other areas of learning which emerge and need to be tackled in the stories and characters and focus attention on them.** (In class MVM 1E (p.32) the need to address concerns of the 'male chauvinistic' attitudes of some members of the class became the focus of the drama originally designed to make Shakespeare's *Twelfth Night* accessible.)

7 – **The innate creativity and the experiences of students, either in the drama-in-education class itself or in classes discussing the projects, need to be encouraged and developed in the dramas and if any of their ideas and suggestions emerge which demonstrate this aspect of the work, the drama needs – at least temporarily – to focus on that aspect of the story even if it does not seem**

to relate to the original aim of the drama or any learning issues that have subsequently evolved. (In discussions on the work on 'The Ideal Society' story of class MVM 2D (p.77), mature married women from another class, called TOPS (see below pp.26 and 78) pointed out that the male students needed to understand that some women need to follow the careers they had before marriage after bearing children and that the husbands should share in the childcare aspect of their life together. This resulted in creating a focus on that problem in the drama.)

8 – **In order to enhance the reality of the dramas, representative props, costumes or some items of costume and some items indicating the setting are provided. Dorothy maintained that we live in a material world and this is especially important to children, so that any abstract elements should be given concrete substance.** (This principle, generally carried out in any case by many teachers in their lessons, was essential in making the dramas real to all the students in this work.)

9 – **Essential learning material for students should consist of universals underlying human experience. Dorothy mentioned Georges Polti's named universal themes in his** *The Thirty Six Dramatic Situations* **and considered that Shakespeare's plays were a rich source of universals.** (The A level and evening class students tested this in their programme Spin-off (see p.94). In my analysis of the themes of each one of Shakespeare's plays they proved to be the source of many universals relating to everyday life).

10 – **The participants in the dramas should always be given praise if their work is good and their self-esteem in what may be a new skill they have acquired, assured.** (This principle is applied generally in education and proved to be essential for the work in this experiment to continue.)

ADDITIONAL FACTORS THAT WERE
NECESSARY TO MAKE THE DRAMAS ACCEPTABLE
TO MOST OF THE STUDENTS

1 – In addition to these aspects of the process, I found that the male craft practice students on apprenticeships as electronic engineers and motor vehicle mechanics needed the dramas to be conducted through the medium of the college television studio. If that was not available to them, filming with a portable camera was essential. Their work involved machines and their respect for the dramas required the use of some kind of machine technology. They were very skilled in the use of any of this equipment and that encouraged them. Also some students were initially unwilling to participate in acting in the dramas so I found it prudent to ask them to become involved in operating the cameras. However, as operating the cameras was a favourite occupation of many of the students, the privilege soon became fairly rotated around the class. Then the participation of every member of the class in the filmed drama itself was considered to be reasonable in order to be 'fair' to all. In order for them to value the film studio and not to take it for granted, I usually only booked sessions in it for one week in three, the other two sessions being taken in their classroom as preparation for the filmed episode.[7]

2 – Another important factor in the use of cameras was that most of them had little experience of live theatre but were used to films, either in cinemas or on TV and they thus were more prepared to participate in a medium familiar to them.

3 – I found that they enjoyed my bringing in properties or costumes which were good to look at, even very valuable, like a silver tea service. It indicated to them that I respected them enough to trust them using such items and was keen to give them pleasure in the presentation of the dramas.

4 – Monitoring the learning effectiveness of the dramas outside of the class was important. This was done in class MVM 1E in 1978–79 (p.32) by a member of staff the result of whose feedback conditioned the content of the following sessions. Another member of staff joined his session of 'Liberal Studies lessons' with class MVM 1E 1979–80 to my adjacent 'English' hour so that we could do monitoring and his acting in role as a team effort. These sessions occurred on the last two periods of a Friday and in spite of the unfavourable time in the college weekly timetable, the students enjoyed them: "Sometimes these lessons are the only ones we go to, Miss," one of them declared.

5 – If members of a class became so involved with the dramas that I could confidently consider them to be hooked on it, I would push the stories into areas which they would normally not accept. For example during the work with class MVM 2D, I pushed the involvement of the students by setting a scene in the gardens of Forty Hall, Enfield, to which we paid an official visit in the college minibus, a college technical lecturer filming scenes in which I costumed one of the actors in exotic dress against banks of flowers (a procedure which they would normally consider to be effeminate but which in this case they totally accepted as a necessary part of their story).

6 – It proved constructive to involve all my varied classes at the college in the dramas in some way, even if it were only discussing the themes with them and getting their opinions on the material. An example of this was the advice given to me (see p.78) by the mature women in a TOPS class about some women's wish for post-marriage continuation of their careers after having children.

7 – I considered that one of the main aims of the process was to encourage students of all the classes to respect themselves and their creative abilities. Often students in some of the craft practice classes were not deemed by some of the staff to have creative faculties or to appreciate art, including theatre (see above p.14 and below p.26). Due to this kind of prejudice which had been

instilled into them, I did not tell the students who were to take part in the filming that the ultimate aim of the filming was to make a Shakespearean play accessible to them. Even when I took classes to see the Theatre Set-Up production of the play, I did not mention that it was a Shakespearean performance. Instead I told them that I was taking them to see a play that had the themes in it that they had been filming in the TV studio. Only when they saw the play's programmes did they understand that they were going to see a play by Shakespeare. They were then chuffed to find that because they had experienced its themes they understood the play, even though the language was sometimes strange to them.

8 – Following the Dorothy Heathcote precept that the content of the filmed sessions would not necessarily be fixed, sometimes the story developed from a framework which the students had devised. An example of this was the session mentioned above (p.81) in class MVM 2D when the open form of the tribunal in 'An Ideal Society' allowed the pupil performing the part of the father to react spontaneously to the suggestions, also given spontaneously, by the student Ali performing a member of the tribunal. In other words, although some preparation for the scenes was done outside the studio, the students held their decision-making tribunal and the resultant conclusions only when filmed 'cold' in the TV studio.

9 – The whole process was introduced to the craft practice classes as a series of TV films which were to be made in episodes in the same way as practised by a professional TV studio. I made it clear that all the films made by all the classes would be seen by other classes at the end of the year, by the Vice Principal of the college and by some professional actors. (I did not tell the students that these actors would be performing roles in the studied play in performances of Theatre Set-Up in order to keep the fact that it was themes from a Shakespearean play that they would be filming secret, thus avoiding what might be a prejudiced negative response). Thus themes of a play explored by one class but not by others would be seen so that many aspects of the Shakespearean play would be seen by all the students. Most importantly, each class became conscious that

they would lose face if their drama work was not taken seriously by them with resultant inadequate films, and would consequently be ridiculed by other classes. The presentation of the films to the Vice Principal would grant them status in the eyes of the college. The involvement of Theatre Set-Up's actors would introduce them to the world of professional theatre into which they had entered in exploring the plays for the ultimate benefit of the interpretation of the plays for the actors. It was also hoped that at least some classes would be able to attend performances by Theatre Set-Up of the play whose themes they had explored, *Twelfth Night* in 1979 and *As You Like It* in 1980. The work with the craft practice students was extended in 1981 to *The Tempest* to be performed in 1982.

THE NATURE OF THE CLASSES WHICH WERE INVOLVED IN THE FILMED DRAMAS

Although all the students that I taught were involved in discussions or role play in the dramas, the only classes involved in the year 1978–79 when *Twelfth Night* was the play to be accessed were those of the part-time motor vehicle mechanic apprentices and the A level drama classes. In the 1979–80 work on *As You Like It*, secretarial and evening drama classes also took part.

MOTOR VEHICLE MECHANIC APPRENTICE AND MECHANICAL ENGINEERING CLASSES

The motor vehicle mechanic and mechanical engineering students were sent on day-release to study at Southgate Technical College for a certain number of hours a week as part of their apprenticeship arrangements with the firms by whom they were employed. They were not ordinary classroom pupils – they were business and work young men. The motor vehicle mechanic apprentices had opportunities to repair cars privately for people and thus they developed a sense of business and economic freedom which gave them a feeling of independence. Thus they objected to the indignity of being returned to a classroom situation at the college, when that was a state for them which had long since been superseded in the reality of their working lives. Some of the young men were married, often with children.

However in the filming process I found that I could draw on their work and business experience and thus reinforce their self-esteem. The environment of the television studio in which we did most of the work, commanded their respect because it resembled their work environment in the sense that it had to be managed properly in order to produce a respected result. Just as a repaired car functioned well, so the reviewed films which they had made gave work-satisfaction.

These young people considered it dishonest to be pretentious in any way, scorning hypocrisy. This made their acting in the films truthful. They often did not want to appear to take themselves too seriously with a resultant reluctance to appear to be too enthusiastic. Peer pressure often conditioned their response to creative work and suppressed the reactions of some of the students who were, in fact, from what, in those days, was considered to be a 'middle class, cultured', background. The usual media through which learning areas were explored in English and Liberal Studies classes were discussion and writing. Many of the mechanics sometimes found these suspect either as symbolising types of people they did not admire – because they considered them to be outside their macho sub-culture – or because they lacked skill themselves in their execution due to educational deprivation. However there were many young people in the classes who were very literate, a fact that I had discovered during the years I was teaching them before I undertook the Dorothy Heathcote-guided work, when I successfully read plays with them in their classes. The students who were very literate tended to ask to read the parts of the characters in the plays and the others enjoyed the outcome of the plots, becoming more literate as they followed the scripts. As long as the plays honoured their macho sub-culture, all the students found them acceptable.[8] I tried, in my subsequent, Dorothy-inspired work with them, to engage all the young people in the classes as participators by developing their skills in drama-in-education as a means of communication, presented to them as an everyday living process.

The group tutors of the mechanics classes could be very supportive of the English and Liberal Studies activities. The young people would lose pay if they did not attend any lessons and were reprimanded if their group tutors complained about them. Some of the mechanics often claimed that they were treated as 'garbage' by members of staff with a resulting low self-respect and rebellious behaviour (see p.67).

BUSINESS STUDIES CLASSES

The Commercial Course 2

This consisted mostly of girls under the age of 19 who did not have to pay for their one-year course in Shorthand and Typewriting, English and Commerce and Office Practice. Entry requirement to the course demanded a selection of passes in GCE or O level exams. Designed for those wishing to do office work as shorthand typists or clerk-typists, the course offered entry to the Royal Society of Arts Secretarial Diploma (stage I) examinations. The girls were competent, industrious, cooperative and always well-mannered.

The TOPS course

This consisted of mature students, mostly women, but with one man, who were eligible for allowances under the Training Opportunities Scheme, with the aim of improving their job prospects. The requirement was that they should be over the age of 19 and that they had been away from full-time education for at least three years. It was an excellent scheme, adequately paid and enthusiastically embraced by its participants who welcomed the chance not only to increase their earning capacity but to expand their general knowledge and creative experience.

DEPARTMENT OF ENGLISH AND LIBERAL STUDIES

A level drama classes

These were students who were taking the drama course as a substitute A level subject, learning skills in acting, and theatre production. There were college theatre productions in which they could participate. A number of these students went on to become professional theatre practitioners but many regarded the course as beneficial for personal development. From 1980 onwards they were able to take the GCSE and A Level Theatre Studies examination courses which had by then newly entered the syllabus. The girls from these classes became experts at acting in role in the Dorothy Heathcote work with the motor vehicle mechanic apprentice students, a skill which some of them furthered in their teaching and acting careers.

Evening class drama classes

These operated on two evenings, one specifically dedicated to the production of plays to be put on in the college and the other designed to develop theatre skills.

I found it beneficial for all concerned to combine the students of all the drama classes in the productions in the college as well as in the Dorothy Heathcote-guided day-time sessions. This rich mix of people gave excellent opportunities for producing adventurous theatre events.

Fig. 2 *The Person who is Ambitious*, Maria (*Twelfth Night*, II. iii.) Forty Hall

CHAPTER TWO

Twelfth Night
(academic year 1978–79)

THEMES OF THE PLAY *TWELFTH NIGHT* ANALYSED IN TERMS OF THEIR UNIVERSAL APPLICATION TO EVERYDAY LIFE

This made them accessible to the students. These are divided into sections suitable for developing into episodes for filming.

1 – **Malvolio and Sir Toby Belch. The outsider.**
- The Killjoy.
- The Killjoy is proved to be a hypocrite.
- Revenge on the hypocrite goes too far.

2 – **Sir Toby Belch and Sir Andrew Aguecheek. The conman and the dupe.**
- A weak person attaches himself to a stronger personality and is conned by that man and his friends.
- They play a trick on him which backfires on themselves.

3 – **Maria and Malvolio. The person who is ambitious but lacks that last edge of status to attain ambition.**
- The person who lives by her/his wits and attains her/his ambition because of this.
- The ambitious person is patronised by a person of authority in the same firm.
- A trick played to make the patronising person a fool.
- Climbing the social ladder.
- A person is rewarded for astuteness by promotion.

4 – "Deceit I see thou art a wickedness." Viola in disguise as a man. Deceit.
- A person pretends to be someone else.
- Situations which arise because people believe this pretence.

5 – The Twins Viola and Sebastian. Mistaken identity.
- A pair of twins move in society unaware of each other's actions.
- Situations which arise when one twin is mistaken for the other.

6 – Orsino's suit of Olivia. The unattainable.
- Wishing for something which is beyond reach.
- Sulking for something which you cannot have.
- Pestering someone for something which they will, or cannot give.
- The hassler.
- The hassler sees someone else get what he wanted for himself.
- Spite against that person.

7 – Orsino and Viola. A situation which you bring upon yourself.
- A disguise entangles a relationship.
- You help someone in achieving something that you wish for yourself.
- In the terms of your job, you must do something which is strongly against your inclinations.
- A role which you adopted to help yourself proves your hindrance.
- You are obliged to persuade someone to accept a job which you want yourself.

8 – Siblings – Viola and Sebastian, Olivia and her dead brother. Affection between siblings.
- Your closest relative or sibling.
- Death of your sibling.
- You take on the characteristics of someone you are very fond of.
- Someone you thought to be dead turns up.

9 – The Fool Feste, Olivia and Fabian. The feeling between employer and employee.

Fig. 3 *Deceit*, Viola in Disguise (*Twelfth Night*, I. v.) Forty Hall

- An old employee seeks re-employment.
- A new employee receives the promotion you had hoped to have.

10 – **Feste and Malvolio. Relationships within a firm.**
- A superior in a firm betrays the wrongdoings of an employee (the squealer).
- Revenge on the squealer.
- An employee is threatened with redundancy due to staleness in his work.

11 – **Antonio and Sebastian. Friendship.**
- Your generosity of friendship puts you into trouble.
- You seem betrayed by the friend on whose behalf you got into trouble.

12 – **Olivia's mourning for her brother, Orsino's suit of Olivia. Self-indulgent emotion. Any over-indulgence in emotion.**
- Mourning – as Olivia.
- Unrequited love – as Orsino.

FILMING WITH CLASS MVM 1E

This English class took place on Fridays at 13.45 hours and had the advantage of being monitored in the following period by the Liberal Studies lecturer, Les, the results of whose questioning of the students determined the content of the drama-in-education sessions. The Dorothy-guided work began at the beginning of the second term in January, the weeks in the first term being taken up with exploring filming techniques in the TV studio.

This class decided to begin preparation on the theme of 'deceit'. They suggested that I should bring a girl into the class and that the deceit should consist of her masquerading as a boy. They had been asking for a whole term for girls to come into the class and here they saw their opportunity. I agreed to ask two of my drama students if they would like to join the class. I suggested two girls as they could support each other in the class, suggesting that one girl could be the dressed-as-a-boy apprentice and the other a secretary in the garage office.

After tossing around several ideas and commenting on issues to do with the sex discrimination act, they decided that the girl would dress up as a boy in order to get a job which was usually considered to be an entirely male province. Although they wished for an occupation outside their sphere of work like coal-mining, they decided that it would be more convenient to make the job the same as their own, an apprentice motor vehicle mechanic. She would dress up as a boy in order to have the same chance of success in her job application as male applicants. The other girl would be a secretary in the garage office. This secretary would reject the advances of all the men in the garage as she fancied the new recruit, unaware that she was a girl. This reflected the *Twelfth Night* story of Olivia falling in love with Viola dressed as a page in the likeness of her brother Sebastian. **Over the years when I was doing this Shakespeare-sourced work, I often found that the boys in these classes hit upon story lines emerging from his themes that Shakespeare himself used in his plays.**

When I pointed out that the class 1C had two girl mechanic apprentices in it they cried out in horror: "We've seen them!"

There followed an interesting discussion of what they considered to be the proper role of women in society and one of the main areas within which exploratory learning might take place emerged. Several boys spoke with disgust of girls who work alongside them at work: "They drink beer!" they exclaimed in horror. When questioned, several of the boys ironically replied that girls are supposed to drink only martinis or sherry.

In his following class, Les asked them: "Well, are they good mechanics? Do they service a car properly, for instance?"

"Oh yes, she's a good mechanic."

"Well what's wrong with her then?"

There began a discussion of their actual views on women's roles, on their own male chauvinism and on the fact that, although they considered this to be socially unacceptable, it seemed inevitable to them:

"Things aren't going to change in our lifetime, Sir."
They told him that they thought a garage was no place for a woman:
"Well, I wouldn't want my wife to work there!" said one.
"Would you like her to work as a glamorous cabaret star in the West End then?" replied Les.
"Certainly not, that wouldn't be decent."
When asked how they expected the girls to dress, they replied that girls were to dress "nicely".
"You mean like you are all dressed now, jumpers, jeans and cords?"
"No, in skirts and blouses, attractively."

When Les told me of this conversation I realised that then we had the practical means through the girls-in-role to vary their dress in the drama-in-education sessions as a way of leading the boys to regarding women as equals. I asked the two girls who had agreed to act in role with the class to come to the first session dressed in their normal student clothing – jeans, trousers and jumpers.

Their entry into the class during the following planning session was met by visible disappointment in their appearance, dressed as they were in casual jeans and jumpers, 'student dress', as the boys themselves were clothed, although we had previously discussed the theme of beautiful clothing being only a 'skin-deep' sort of thing.

It was decided that the apprentice Mick would be the boss of the garage and that Lorraine would play his disguised girlfriend. They had decided that the disguised girl should be engaged to the boss and that he would not recognise her as a boy. (Confusion would later occur one day at work when she forgot to conceal the engagement ring that he had given her.) After working at the garage for a while, she would cause the other mechanics in the garage to be jealous as she was better at the job than they were, thus attracting praise from the boss and attention from the secretary whom they all fancied. They decided that her disguise would be blown when she would weep at being falsely accused of a misdemeanour at work added to which her cap would fall off and her long girl hair would fall down. In order to avoid being considered to be socially unacceptable male chauvinists, the boys elected to make the story end with her being accepted as a female motor vehicle mechanic.

They divided the story into the five episodes that we could film in the TV studio:

1 – Scene: a restaurant. The boss and his fiancée are at one table. The boss mentions that there is a vacancy for an apprentice mechanic at this garage. She is to ask if he would consider a female applicant. He will answer that he would not as it would cause too much trouble among his other male employees. The secretary (who could not see the face of the fiancée) and one of the garage employees are seated at another table. They comment on the boss and his fiancée.
2 – The interview for the job. There are two finalists, the fiancée and male applicant in the practical test which will decide the successful candidate. The fiancée wins, the boss not recognising her.
3 – Scene: the garage workshop. The fiancée is being teased by the men in the garage who are jealous of the success she is making of her job and by the fact that the secretary fancies her above them.
4 – The restaurant. The boss expresses concern about not knowing the job situation of his fiancée.
5 – Acceleration of the problems at the workshop when the fiancée weeps, her cap falls off and her true identity is revealed.

When Les asked the boys about the entry of the girls into the class they expressed their disappointment: "They're not real girls, Sir. They dress like us!"

For the next planning session with the class I asked the girls to dress in more feminine dress, skirts and blouses. When they entered the room, the boys were delighted.

We planned the first restaurant scene, the learning to be explored becoming restaurant etiquette and style. From the class came all the correct points concerning the way a waiter should serve and some interesting points from one boy for the style of the restaurant:

"Silver, lace, candles and a slim vase in the middle of the table containing a single rose."

The silver and lace of this suggestion implied that it was a fantasy vision of an elegant restaurant!

However I was happy to realise the boy's dream-restaurant and supplied these for the filmed restaurant scene. In addition I decided to costume the girls in the story in the way that the boys would like to see them and gave them some strappy black evening dress costumes to wear. When the boys came into the TV studio to make the filmed episode they were astounded. The lights were dimmed and the two tables were decked with lace table cloths, silver vases and roses so that the appearance of the studio was transformed into the elegant restaurant they had hoped for. Sitting at the tables were these two glamorous creatures in elegant black evening dresses whom the boys hardly recognised from the first time they had seen the girls in their student clothes. By commanding their respect by dressing in ways which demonstrated their potential as the females the boys wanted them to be, they made it clear that as fellow students of the college dressed in student-type clothes, they were not only inherently beautiful women, but the equal of male students with the right to dress appropriately. From that moment on the girls could work with the mechanics without any problems with their image and in the next sessions they could return to dressing in their student clothes.

This and previous episodes demonstrated the effectiveness of the Dorothy Heathcote-guided drama-in-education method of promoting learning by creating scenarios from life with real props and costumes to give ideas a material substance. So relaxed were the girls with the boys in the class after this that during the tea and lunch breaks in the college refectory, they often joined the boys on the days when they attended the college. This was a considerable achievement as in the social order of the college, students from different departments rarely mixed with each other.

There was still a problem to be tackled with the behaviour of one of the boys, Costos, who from the moment the girls entered the class had tried to flirt with them in an impolite way. This was tackled in the next filmed episode of the job interview in which the fiancée was tested for mechanical expertise by the boss who would not recognise her. Costos was cast as one of the garage mechanics who would hassle the new recruit to the firm. By this time he had become embarrassed about his behaviour to the girls whom he now recognised as students of the college just like himself. I urged him to be more aggressively chauvinistic which ironically he then found difficult, his voice emerging in little more than a whisper!

The planning of the episode in which the fiancée should be unmasked was strange. Their ideas were brilliant, suggestions being fluent and perceptive, but their behaviour was atrocious and they caused bedlam in the classroom, with complaints from members of staff in nearby rooms. It seemed to me that they were over-excited, realising that they were doing something unusual for them and doing it well.

By now Peter, one of the students, had become expert at directing the filming from the control room of the TV studio which left me free to work in the performance section. In the next filmed scenario the ring which the boss had given to his fiancée accidentally fell out of her pocket. The boss accused her of stealing and pushed her. Her cap fell off, her hair fell down and he recognised her. The boys decided that they would accuse her of being a lesbian. I told them that that was a situation which had already occurred in reality with the class MVM 1C that week and that the girl mechanic involved had successfully quashed that (see below p.42). During the period of time this work was being done, society was generally homophobic, and same-sex relationships, certainly among these young people, both male and female, were not regarded sympathetically. In the context of the work done with these motor vehicle mechanic apprentice classes there was the added prejudice against women doing what was considered to be the men's work of practising as engineers or mechanics. Consequently any women choosing to work in those fields were considered to have the male characteristics which were mistakenly attributed to women who were lesbians. It was my aim of sessions with classes displaying this attitude to credit women with the natural ability, regardless of their gender, to be engineers or mechanics. (When I look at the discrimination shown regarding the nature of lesbians in the classes whose work is recorded herein, I find it commendable that the decades intervening between the era this work with the mechanic apprentices was being done and the present when it is being written up, have seen considerable progress in the understanding of same-sex relationships to the point of legalising marriage between them in many countries.)

The girl playing the role of the fiancée had decided to tell the boss that she had adopted the role in order to be with him at work and that she no longer wished to be a mechanic but would take a more conventionally feminine job and would look forward to being his wife. This reflected the *Twelfth Night* story whose plot lines the girls and I had tried to imply throughout the filming in order to prepare the boys to understand and enjoy the Theatre Set-Up performance of the play later in the year. As well as preparing the boys for an understanding of *Twelfth Night*, the sessions had created life-learning in the acceptance of women as equals of men, the boys had successfully proved themselves capable of being creative in suggesting scenarios on a given theme and acting them out in dramas which they had filmed themselves, and they had done so by acting as a team.

In the following sessions the boys viewed not only all the episodes that they had successfully made, but also those of the other motor vehicle apprentice classes. The class were able to compare their work with that of other classes and they saw all the themes that had been treated by analogy from *Twelfth Night*. Only four of the boys were able to come to the Theatre Set-Up performance of the play but they were very gratified to be able to understand and enjoy it.

FILMING WITH CLASS MVM 1C

The class took place at 16.15 hours on a Thursday. The lateness of the time in the day was a problem as everyone was tired, but the sessions had the advantage in the participation of a member of staff, John, who took the previous lesson in which he could monitor the process from the preceding week. He also volunteered to act in role for some of the episodes.

The class MVM 1C was different from any other motor vehicle mechanic apprentice class at Southgate Technical College at that time in that it included two girl apprentices. They were placed in that class because among the other apprentices were a greater number with higher academic qualifications than had ever attended the college before. The subject of 'male chauvinism' and women's roles in society were therefore to be initially avoided because it was a real

Fig. 4 *The Conman and the Dupe*, Sir Toby Belch and Sir Andrew Aguecheek (*Twelfth Night*, II. iii.) Forty Hall

issue and too 'near the bone'. The boys in this class did not take kindly to the girls, did not treat them equally, and gave them a bad time on the course until they became used to them. As the girls felt self-conscious I decided initially to keep their role in the project behind camera, working in the control room. They willingly acceded to this suggestion.

This class selected to begin by preparing the theme about Sir Toby Belch and Sir Andrew Aguecheek – the conman and the dupe.

1 – A weak person attaches himself to a stronger personality and is conned by that man and his friends.
2 – They play a trick on him which backfires on themselves.

They selected a casino as the ideal location for setting up a group of conmen and their dupe. The boys proved willing to take parts in the drama, possibly because it involved activities they respected such as playing cards, drinking and smoking. We managed to involve all the members of the class in activities, either behind or in front of the camera.

After the classroom preparation they filmed the first episode which they set in an anteroom in their casino. I brought in whisky bottles filled with water and they smoked real cigarettes. The 'dupe' bought all the drinks and was promised that they would 'show him the ropes' of successful gambling. In the second filmed episode the 'dupe' was conned of his money. Apart from the central theme of exploitation of the weak, the only areas within which learning might take place that evolved were card playing and team work. This last was quite good. They established in the studio that my forte was not as a television director, so they took over all the planning of the camera shots themselves. They also planned most of the action. I only interfered when the arguments started and I took decisions in terms of "what will be good television". In the second episode they had complete control of the filming and the action to be filmed and I was only the floor manager, signalling to the actors the cue to begin. Continuing the principle of deepening belief in the process by having relevant props, we had outdated chips supplied by a croupier friend of mine. This made the scenario more authentic for the students.

They filmed two scenes, in the first allowing the 'dupe' to win two games and in the second conning him of all his money. An outside person, the casino detective, who would have been watching the games on closed circuit television, was then brought in to intervene in the next episode to save the conman, restoring his lost cash, sacking the corrupt croupier and forbidding his 'mates' to ever return to the casino. This session lasted for two hours, my lesson being combined with the previous one.

The students were justifiably very pleased with the standard of their filming when they reviewed all the episodes at the end of this last session. They had just achieved a remarkable phenomenon – a two-hour unbroken stretch of concentrated work in Liberal Studies which was an almost unheard-of thing! Their weariness showed, but their satisfaction with their work compensated for this.

They were ready for more filming and the lecturer, John, who had taken them for the previous hour, decided to combine his hour with mine and join in the dramas in role. I gave him the choice of themes and he selected the Malvolio-Feste theme in which a superior (the squealer) in a firm betrays the wrongdoings of another employee. My aim was to test the creative capacity of the class and their powers to sustain energy and interest although tired, by doing a whole series of preparation and filming of several episodes within the two-hour period. John was hoping for additional learning to take place regarding industrial relations, particularly the possibility of corruption in industry and how to deal with it.

Robin, a boy who, because of much absence had not become socially adjusted to the girls in the class, had become fascinated with the theme of the episode and made many suggestions. I had offered him the role of the employee betrayed by the squealer. Aware that he was cooperating with me to a degree that he thought (inaccurately) would cause him to lose face before his peers, he accused the girls of being lesbians (see above p.37). I immediately asked one of the girls, Jill, to go into role as his girlfriend in order to defend herself. The class had decided that the squealer should betray Robin from jealousy and revenge as he was having an affair with the squealer's wife.

An amazing scene occurred during the filming of a scene between Jill and Robin. Robin exploited the situation to show off and began to fondle Jill. However she called his bluff and fondled him back. There was a roar of approval from the rest of the class. She did more to command the respect of the boys for girl mechanics in that one bold action than all the posturing of arguments could have done. Later when I was complimenting her on her sporting spirit, she said contemptuously: "Call me a lesbian!" (See above p.37.)

At the end of the two-hour session, the class had prepared, planned and filmed a series of three episodes and they were highly pleased with themselves. I was correspondingly satisfied with the experiment which had tested the power of the filmed drama-in-education to stretch a class already exhausted at the end of the day.

This class still had the motivation to film another episode, choosing the part of the theme concerning Maria and Malvolio which represented the latter deceived into appearing before Olivia cross-gartered and in yellow stockings and which they entitled 'The Fool'. In their interpretation of the story, a foolish newly employed person would be gulled by his workmates into going to an interview with the boss in a ridiculous way in the belief that he would be pleased. This included performing a song-and-dance routine as a result of which the boss would sack him.

The Vice Principal of the college agreed to come into the studio to view with the boys the films that the class had made. He was genuinely pleased and surprised at their invention of theme and dialogue. He appreciated that the TV work had monitored their real abilities and shown their qualities of integrity and imagination for which many (including himself) at Southgate Technical College had not given motor vehicle mechanic apprentices credit.

Sadly the distances of their workplaces from Forty Hall, Enfield were too great to enable them to see the Theatre Set-Up production of *Twelfth Night* but I considered that the filming had justified itself in terms of the learning that had taken place and the visible boost to the students' self-esteem.

Fig. 5 *The Outsider*, Malvolio and Sir Toby Belch (*Twelfth Night*, III. iv.) inside Forty Hall

Fig. 6 *Relationships within a Firm*, The Fool and Malvolio (*Twelfth Night*, II. v.) Forty Hall

FILMING WITH CLASS MVM 1A

The class took place on Mondays at 14.15 hours. There was a conflict in this class between high ability and fluency of imagination and the cynicism and rudeness which some boys considered denotes loyalty to their peer and social groups. The latter attitude was epitomised by the boy, Martin, who on the first day of the class put his head on the desk and objected to our interrupting his attempts to sleep. From that point he was consistently rude until my drama student, Sally, "modified his behaviour". A large group of boys, David, Chris, Leo, Sav and Harry, were cooperative and worked well. Several boys, like Ricky and Peter, oscillated between attitudes. Ricky was one of the main contributors of ideas for the programmes and was part of the cast for the first episode and yet it seemed important to him to project an image of unwillingness to cooperate – he would not go into the second episode. Peter took part in the second episode but protested against further participation. There was an incident of staff lack of cooperation wherein a member of staff took out a student who was key to the filming from what he considered to be "useless Liberal Studies" to do extra work on maths.

The class chose to film their first episodes (about the relationship between Malvolio and Sir Toby Belch) – 'The Outsider'.

Episode 1. The killjoy
      2. The killjoy proved a hypocrite
      3. Revenge on the hypocrite which goes too far

The episodes represented a good learning area to explore – industrial relations. They set the scene in a television studio. In the first episode two employees were reprimanded by their boss for chewing gum in the studio; in the second episode the boss himself was to be seen chewing gum. An argument would ensue concerning the respective rights of employers and employees, in which the employees claimed that restrictions imposed on them should be observed by the management. The boss would reply by telling them that if they wanted to keep their jobs they would have to do as they were told.

The next episode was planned. A strike of the employees against the management was decided upon. In order to create a more cooperative class atmosphere, I decided to tackle the rebellious element in the class by imposing on them attitudes which they consider symptomatic of protest against the establishment. I arranged for most of the class to be in the scene – all on strike against the management in a rebellious mob, while the boss tries to remonstrate with them and get them to run the studio. The most common action to signal revolt in these classes was the displaying of a nude female photograph on page three of *The Sun* newspaper. I therefore insisted that when they were on strike in the film they should all bring pornographic magazines and beer bottles and display page three of *The Sun*. When this episode was later filmed along with the previous and later ones, the point was made to the difficult students in the class that management could upstage their behaviour, decreasing its effectiveness. The cooperative members of the class implied in the next episode that unwarranted rebellion was self-defeating when they created a scenario of the loss of all the employees' jobs with the closure of the studio, caused by the strike. However a stronger tool against rebellious rudeness was soon introduced into the class in the form of two of my drama class girls!

The class chose to begin another topic about the confusion in *Twelfth Night* caused by the twins, Viola and Sebastian – 'Mistaken Identity – the Twins'. We had access to primary experience in the class of this topic as one of the boys, David, was an identical twin. They decided to have one person play both twins. No one would volunteer to act this part and I could not do it as well as direct the stage action so I promised to ask several girl drama students to come into the class. Sally and Frieda agreed to do this, with Sally acting both twins and Frieda playing different roles as required throughout the episodes. Sally would reform the hitherto rude Martin, involving him in the filming as the boyfriend of herself as the bad twin. It reinforced my conviction that in-role girls of roughly the same age as the boys were the best at creating the learning in the kind of drama-in-education that we were carrying out at Southgate College!

The ideas for situations which would arise from mistaken identity flowed fast. The students decided that one twin would be impatient, bad-tempered, rude and of generally bad character. The other twin would be patient, kindly and of good character. We divided ourselves within the class into those who were patient and those who were impatient and I decided that the learning area that might be explored might be "diplomacy".

The students arranged the episodes into these situations:

1 – In a restaurant. The bad twin would complain of bad service, leaving in disgust, having caused a waiter to lose his job. When the good twin comes into the restaurant she is refused service.
2 – A court case. The bad twin commits a traffic offence and the good twin is arrested for it. Eventually the court must dismiss both twins as they cannot decide who committed the crime. (Martin suggested that the bad twin should be arrested while sitting on his knee. Now, due to the lovely Sally's influence, agreeing to participate in the filming, he cooperated fully and many laughs were had in the planning of his scenes with her. During the filming of the first episode with her his performance was very good, his improvised speech fluent and relevant to the subject.)
3 – Both twins apply for the same job and both lose because offence is created by the confusion over their identities.
4 – The eventual break-up of the sisters. The good twin can take no more. An argument (to be contrived by split-screen techniques of filming a telephone conversation) takes place.

The students debated how the good twin would finish the relationship. "Have her face remodelled" was the favourite suggestion.

At this point the final episode of the previous theme, 'The Outsider', was filmed, the students very pleased with the result of that whole series.

However only one more session was possible in the TV studio due to booking confusion. This was very sad as there had been much excitement over the job-interview episode. Ricky, wishing to show off, had suggested that the job would be that of a club hostess. Following Dorothy's advice to take everything that they said seriously and to give a material reality to any setting, I agreed with this suggestion, asking my croupier friend to supply us with outdated gambling chips. Wishing for students to take more responsibility for the process of the filming, the member of staff in charge of the control room and I were deliberately weak at selecting camera angles. This motivated two of the students to volunteer to do this. They felt too self-conscious to admit this action before their peers so we discussed the preparation of the future episodes in the studio after the class had left. Evidently they had been waiting for some time for the right opportunity to make the offer to me of assistance.

Lack of cooperation from some members of the College staff sabotaged the future of the drama-in-education learning with this class. Not only was the TV studio never made available again, being booked up by staff teaching 'sensible' subjects but I was denied access to the students' phone numbers which I needed to invite them to see the performance of *Twelfth Night*.[1] However some of the members of this class returned to me as students of Liberal Studies in the class MVM 2D in the following academic year, 1979–80, so that I was able to continue working with them. As Sally was no longer available they could not finish the filming of the previous year's episodes, but they went on to do other work whose standards, both technically and conceptually, were excellent so they ultimately received the satisfaction not granted from the previous year's work.

Fig. 7 *The Brothers*, Orlando protests to Old Adam about his brother's mistreatment of him (*As You Like It*, I. i.) Forty Hall

CHAPTER THREE

As You Like It
(academic year 1979–80): class MVM1E

THEMES OF THE PLAY *AS YOU LIKE IT* ANALYSED IN TERMS OF THEIR UNIVERSAL APPLICATION TO EVERYDAY LIFE

These are divided into sections suitable for developing into episodes for filming.

1 - **The younger Duke usurps the court of the older Duke.**
   The takeover.
   - One group takes over or dispossesses another.
   - The two groups intermix to their mutual advantage.

2 - **The changed material culture within the Forest of Arden.**
   The takeover of a style of dress or living.
   - One group adopts the style of dress of another.
   - Different attitudes to this are reflected.

3 - **The Duke Frederick's behaviour towards Orlando and Rosalind.**
   Prejudice.
   - A person usurps a job from somebody, probably by blackmail.
   - A person does not give credit or reward where it is due.
   - An employer unfairly dismisses someone from employment.
   - As a result of this the employer loses the respect of his family and employees.

4 - **Charles the Wrestler. The boasting boxer or anyone boasting that they will succeed.**

- The boxer boasts that he will easily defeat his opponent or someone boasts that they are going to succeed.
- They lose.

5 – **Rosalind disguised as a man. Disguise.**
- Someone adopts a disguise.
- This causes harm to others.

6 – **The 'Golden Age' society of the Duke and his followers in the Forest of Arden. The Ideal Society.**
- An ideal society is created.
- Its ideals are tested.

7 – **The ex-courtiers in the Forest of Arden have an ideal ruler in the Duke just as he was when reigning in his Dukedom. The King.**
- The principle of monarchy is selected by the people of an African country by referendum.
- The chosen king is threatened by republican terrorists who seize the government.
- Mercenaries are hired by the monarchists to restore the king to his throne by defeating the terrorist leaders and overthrowing their government.
- The king is crowned in a ceremony wherein he affirms his people's political ideals.

8 – **Touchstone wins Audrey from William but Silvius wins Phebe from Rosalind disguised as Ganymede. The flash guy and the steady.**
- The flash guy takes the girl away from the steady.
- Sometimes the steady wins the girl.

9 – **Oliver and Orlando, the two Dukes. Brothers.**
- There is a quarrel between two brothers, and the elder arranges a fight for the younger, hoping that he will be killed.
- The fight takes place before a gang leader who is not pleased when the younger brother seems to have killed his henchman.
- The gang leader's sister and girlfriend watch the fight and the

girlfriend falls in love with the younger brother.
- The younger brother escapes to a faraway country.
- He meets the gang leader's sister and her friend who have also escaped from the gang leader to that country.
- The elder brother is victimised by the gang leader, escapes to the faraway country, is saved from danger by his brother and falls in love with the gang leader's sister.
- The gang leader relents when it is discovered that his henchman did not die, and the two couples are married.

10 – **'Melancholy Jaques'. The outsider.**
- The outsider is responsible for the planned action of a gang.
- Violence occurs which he does not approve of.
- He is killed or ousted by his fellow gang members who fear his loyalty.

11 – **Oliver, Orlando, Old Adam, Jaques De Boys, Duke Frederick. The family firm or enterprise.**
- The younger brother in a family firm complains to his brothers that he is not given enough responsibility.
- He threatens to leave and is supported by the firm's technical manager who introduces him into another firm.
- His brothers experience financial difficulties as a small firm from competition threatened by a larger.
- The brothers suggest amalgamation with the firm the younger brother has joined in order to face this threatened competition.

12 – **Rosalind as Ganymede. Disguise.**
- A girl disguises herself as a man in order to pilot a spaceship.
- Her presence on board creates confusion.

13 – **The shepherd Corin and the pretend shepherds, Rosalind and Celia. The real and the pseud.**
- A group of people pretend to be what they are not.
- They are cheated of their money by someone who actually is what they are pretending to be.

CLASS MVM 1E

The class took place on Friday at 16.15, a very unfavourable time of day as the students were usually tired.

This class was entirely different from the previous year's MVM 1E but contained a student, Amadeo, from that year's MVM 1E group. The boys seemed quite young and were not cynical or rude. They chose to begin their filming on the theme 'the takeover'. In *As You Like It* the main takeover is the possession of the Forest of Arden by the Duke and his followers and by Rosalind, Celia, Touchstone, Oliver and Orlando. They have all been dispossessed themselves, yet they occupy territory belonging to the deer of the forest (which they kill for food) and the local farmers upon whose lives they make a considerable impact. The Duke and Jacques are aware of this anachronism (II, 1, 21–30). Touchstone dispossesses the local farmer, William, of his would-be-wife, Audrey, but although Silvius is temporarily dispossessed of the affections of Phebe who falls in love with Rosalind disguised as a man, he gains her as a wife, at the insistence of Rosalind when her disguise is lifted.

It is a theme explored by Shakespeare in many of its aspects, sometimes the takeover being to the advantage of the local folk (the shepherd Corin is given continued employment by Rosalind and Silvius gains his wife) and sometimes disadvantageous (William loses Audrey, the deer in the forest their lives).

I promised the boys that initially I would bring in some drama girls to work with them. Jenny and Katharine volunteered, acting in role as characters analogous to Audrey and Phebe. The class decided that the takeover would be of social dominance in a pub; that the group called the 'Takeover' should have been dispossessed of their own pub by its being rebuilt; that two of the Takeover group should be scouting for a new pub for the whole group; that Jenny and Katharine should be the bored and dissatisfied girlfriends of Neil and John of the 'local' group patronising the pub; and that the two 'scouts' of the Takeover should chat up the two girls who would go off with them, leaving the local boys swilling beer and playing darts.

When this episode was filmed the boys were very impressed by the expertise of the girls and they cooperated with them in the acting and filming. The member of staff in charge of the TV studio was very pleased with their general demeanour. There was an element in this class of yearning for sophistication which I hoped to work on and possibly satisfy.

There was no evidence of that, however in the following episodes which the class planned. The next episode would involve the whole of the class divided into locals and Takeovers. For the episode to have dramatic form, the focal point of conflict would be the recorded music that was to be played in the pub. Amadeo was to be the disc jockey, sitting at a table and playing records as requested. When the Takeover group who were superior in numbers would enter, they would declare the music being played to be rubbish and would insist that their own records were played. Conflict would result. This episode was successfully filmed and the next featured revenge of the locals upon the Takeovers. As they had decided that the landlord of the pub was the father of one of the locals, they planned that he would support their claim that the Takeovers, in revenge for the theft of the locals' girlfriends and their bullying over the music, would not be allowed to have any drinks in his pub. The Takeovers would decide that drink was more important than music and they would concede to the locals. In the subsequent filming I was pleased that a mixing of the two groups had begun. This led to the main learning area now coming into focus about cliques and group chauvinism. I wished to create a happening within which it would be realised that a 'shot of new blood into the system' could be beneficial.

We began planning an episode in which the advantages of mixing the two groups would be manifested. The realms within which this should take place were employment, hobbies, club membership and holidays. However a new and exciting topic emerged which the students wished to pursue: different occupations.[1]

After a discussion about what careers they might have preferred to follow rather than their present one, they planned several innovative ways in which persons from one group were able to help those from the other.

A boy from one group:

a – Is enabled to get an entry into the building trade through the family connections of the other group.
b – Can go horse riding on the horse belonging to a friend of the other group.
c   Membership of a particular club is guaranteed by being sponsored by a member of the other group.
d – Wishing to go on an adventure holiday, the boy is able to join several boys from the other group.

The ideas and filming were done with enthusiasm and skill in both verbal improvisation and technical competence.

Filming was prepared for the final episode of this series – the wedding of the two girls (representing Audrey and Phebe in *As You Like It)*. This would have to be done without the presence of the A level Drama students who were no longer interested in performing in role with the class.[2] The mechanics students came up with ideal solutions to this problem, deciding, much to my pleasure that they had acquired this skill, of representing the action. They did this by conveying the storylines through telephone calls and through a related scene – a stag party.

The next theme which the class worked on, was blessed by the member of staff, Ciaran, who took the previous Liberal Studies lesson, joining with us for the two sessions and playing in role for the class. In order to further stretch their imaginations, I had decided to ask them to extend their previous theme, 'the takeover' into 'the takeover of an idea'. They liked the challenge this presented and chose to base the episodes on conflicts over dress in differing groups who were members of the same club. The groups would be:

a – The Classics, distinguished by formal dress.
b – The Alcs, dressed informally.
c – The New Wave, dressed casually.

They initiated the theme of 'the takeover' by planning and filming action in which members of the Classics group entered the club dressed casually in the style of the New Wave as they found their formal dress uncomfortable and needed to relax. In order to enjoy the relaxation afforded by their casual dress they would be prepared to endure any opposition from the New Wave group. In the filming of this episode, unlike other classes who preferred to work the cameras and the controls, they declared their commitment to the performance element of the dramas. When I offered to several of them to work at the controls, they said, "No, we'll stick with the acting, Miss."

The activity they selected going on within the club to which the different groups belonged was a club for the meeting of film-makers, screen writers and actors with the Classics as the actors, the New Wave the film-makers and the Alcs the screen writers. As I belonged to a professional theatre council I described to them what its meetings were like and the very evident differences between the style of managers, writers and actors. They planned and filmed the following episode skilfully, mixing up tolerant and intolerant attitudes to the Classic members dressed casually. Some were denied professional employment by intolerant New Wave and Alcs members while others supported them. Thus they demonstrated learning concerning toleration of diversity and new ideas.

Eager to continue with more filming, the class decided to tackle the theme 'prejudice'. The episodes of the prejudiced person were entitled:

1 – He usurps a job from somebody. Probably by blackmail.
2 – He does not give credit or reward where it is due.
3 – He unfairly dismisses someone from employment.
4 – He loses the respect and services of his own family and employees.

The class decided that Tony (who is black), should be the cause of the prejudice.[3] As there were no other black students in the class his role as boss would be untenable so he decided to be the victim. Evidently, regardless of race, the boys identified strongly with this theme as they often felt victimised at work. For this reason they chose to set the series in a garage.

They planned and filmed a very successful series in which Tony, who had excelled in his work and service to the garage, was not given the promotion he deserved, the job he should have had being given to another employee who had blackmailed the boss over his malpractice in the garage, 'ringing' cars (that is disguising stolen cars by transferring their number plates). In disgust at the boss's treatment of Tony all the mechanics employed in the garage left and formed their own very efficient garage under Tony's leadership. The series might be considered to have exorcised the mechanics' resentment at the victimisation they considered that they suffered at work. In their resolution of the story in which all the members of the garage supported the victim and left to form their own successful garage, they may have been carrying out wishful thinking with regard to their own work situations. In this respect this might have been of benefit for them and the drama-in-education work may have helped them psychologically.

There was then only one possible filming session available before the end of the academic year and the class decided that they would like to make a variation of the Charles the Wrestler versus Orlando wrestling match which they called 'The Boasting Boxer'. I explained that filming this would be difficult as we did not have the facilities or expertise to stage a boxing match in our TV studio. Their solution to this pleased me as they had by then acquired skills in representing action and they presented the episode as recounted in a telecast-reported session by one of the boys who would also interview the combatants before the match. They had fun with filming the contrast between the boasting boxer who would lose and the modest one who would win.

We subsequently viewed all the films which the boys had made during the year and they were justifiably proud of their work. Unfortunately they did not receive the benefit due to them in being able to see *As You Like It* at Forty Hall as their group tutor denied me access to their work phone numbers. I resolved that in the future I would bypass this negative staff attitude by requesting the students to give me the appropriate phone numbers while we were in class together.

Fig. 8 *The Boasting Boxer*, Charles the Wrestler (*As You Like It*, I. ii.) Chaplaincy Gardens, Isles of Scilly

Fig. 9 *Prejudice,* (losing the respect of his own family) Duke Frederick against Rosalind and Orlando. His daughter, Celia, leaves her father and pledges to accompany Rosalind into exile (*As You Like It*, I. ii.) Forty Hall

CHAPTER FOUR

As You Like It:
classes MCC 2A and MVM 3C

CLASS MCC 2A

These students were not motor vehicle mechanic apprentices. They were on day-release from their firms to further their studies in mechanical engineering. I took them for one and a half hours every Monday for the subject of General Studies. The first theme they chose to film was on Melancholy Jaques, 'the outsider', in which one member of the group is more perceptive and sensitive than the others and is ostracised because of it. They set the action within a gang of young people all of whom for fun were given nicknames: Tony (the brains of the outfit) was 'The Professor', Carl 'Zulu', Matthew 'Fishy', Paul 'Curly', Mark 'Poser', Steve 'Stiffy', Chris 'Alo', and Mike 'Bulk'. The gang would be involved in petty crime.

Their first episode involved the planning of robbing a shop. During a game of cards The Professor would tell the gang his plan for this enterprise but would object when Zulu insisted that Fishy's suggested use of violence be carried out to ensure the plan's success. The TV studio was very pleased with the technical standards of the class's filming of this episode, especially when the overhead mirror was used to show the card game!

The next episodes to be filmed showed the results of the robbery. Unlike the rest of the gang who were pleased with the raid, The Professor would be very depressed as an old man who had been the watchman had been killed during the raid and when he would declare his intention of leaving the gang, Zulu would kill him as he feared that he would betray the gang. I found their decision to kill Tony's character interesting. Part of the reason for that, I felt, was that Tony was in fact, different from the others and they objected to it. I thus found that one of the uses of this episode was to provide a catharsis (meaning in this context a means through which feelings can be safely released) for the objection of the class to Tony's separateness from them. It was all done in a very good-natured way. There was also an element of jealousy as Tony was also considered to be handsome as well as different. I find it difficult to define the way in which Tony was different. There was a sense about him that things would always go well for him.

My requests for toleration of the 'different' person were all refused. In *As You Like It* Melancholy Jaques, although ridiculed by his companions, is regarded as a source of entertainment and his decision to leave the Court, although regretted, is not refused.

Carl had all the ideas for the next episodes which the class decided would be on the theme of the conflict between Orlando (with Adam's support) and Oliver, in the setting of a recording firm, the three black boys in the class representing the brothers. Terry, the youngest brother, would protest that he was not being given any opportunity for management or solo singing. Renos, the technical manager of the firm would introduce Terry to another firm who would take him on as a solo singer and director. This setting for the episodes was good as it gave the students the opportunity to explore an occupation outside their particular field of engineering. The filming of these episodes was unfortunate as the TV studio was out of action, filming had to be done outside with the Sony Rover camera and the class behaviour was so bad that I complained to their group tutor to have them officially reprimanded. The incident demonstrated that they could not handle freedom. I subsequently decided that their everyday work was so regimented that the General Studies period represented a release from this. I needed to structure some kind of release into the film sessions.

Chastened, in the next session they watched the films that they had already made: "Are we the best at making films, Miss?"

When we were able to return to the repaired TV studio, order prevailed again. This demonstrated the beneficial power that the studio had over the students who respected it, whereas filming outside was (as they declared): "Just a giggle, Miss!"

Part of the problem was that in the TV studio everyone had a job to do with tasks in the control room and operating the cameras in the acting studio as well as involvement in acting out the stories. **I truly believe that should basic TV studios like this be provided in districts with young people who become delinquent in their behaviour, and filming in this nature with them be carried out, their creative skills would be appreciated, they would become absorbed in the work and thrive. The cost would be compensated by less expense than that needed to officially reprimand them and often, at great financial expense, incarcerate them.**

The exotic setting for the next series of 'Disguise' was a spacecraft.[1] Sally, one of the A level students experienced at acting in role with the mechanics classes volunteered to work with the class who decided that she would be disguised as a male astronaut as the enterprise running the spacecraft did not employ females. Her fiancée, Tony, was to be a member of the crew. The student Grant devised a complex plot. He suggested that there would be on board an enemy alien who would have set off alarms when the security systems detected the chemical leak with which he hoped to disable the spacecraft. The alarms would also have detected Sally. When she was found she was unconscious from the chemical leak, her space helmet would be removed to attend to her and her female identity would be revealed.

The filming of this episode was difficult as Sally was not available but the class showed their initiative in inventing ways around that. They also changed the look of the studio by unwinding the rolls of corrugated cardboard around the room to give the impression of different sections of the spacecraft. I felt that this series and this episode in particular were giving the boys a chance to 'play' as if they were much younger. It seemed that this was what they needed and would be of more service to them psychologically than a strict format to the lesson.

They then planned the detection of the on-board 'alien' who would actually be an android, designed by the organisers of the space mission to be able to resist problems in interspace travel which could not be tolerated by humans. When the crew detected him they planned to destroy him, but then a mechanical failure occurred in the spacecraft which only he could fix and they then understood his function on board. Tony suggested that he would feel insecure that an android could do more than he could, he would have a nervous breakdown and Sally would minister to him. The class strongly disapproved of this: "It has no story, Miss!" they all complained.

So they decided that when Sally's female identity was discovered Tony would wish her to stay on board as crew but the rest of the crew said that they would only accept that if he accepted the android. This version of events was successfully filmed.

One of my secretarial students, Sonya, agreed to act in role for the class in their selected theme of 'the real and the pseud', to be performed in a casino night club where Carl, a playboy, would take advantage of a group of very naive and clumsy boys who would enter the night club, boasting of their non-existent past money-winning experiences. Sonya dressed in a black evening dress and acted most effectively in role.

There was much good discussion in the class about pretension and the relative merits of aspiring to a lifestyle beyond one's present mode of living, or of being always true to an understated self-image. No conclusions were reached but Carl reflected the class bias towards the latter policy in his ultimate treatment of the pretending 'hypocrite' boys whom he considered merited punishment for their hypocrisy.

Much fun was had in the filming with the crass behaviour of the hypocrite boys, in mishandling the restaurant crockery and cutlery, calling out to the girls in the club as if they were street urchins and trying to chat up Sonya. Carl 'punished' the hypocrites by winning all their money and successfully chatting up Sonya.

A number of these boys came to a dress rehearsal of *As You Like It* at Forty Hall, enjoying seeing the themes in the play that all the classes, including themselves, had filmed, and thereby understanding and enjoying the play.

Fig. 10 *Disguise*, Rosalind (*As You Like It*, IV. i.)
Tresco Abbey Gardens, Isles of Scilly

Fig. 11 *The Flash Guy and the Steady*, Touchstone courts Audrey (*As You Like It*, III. iii.) Forty Hall

CLASS MVM 3C

This group was very difficult to deal with at the beginning of their course. This was their third year at the College and they claimed that they had been treated as "garbage" by the Liberal Studies staff for the previous two years and could not believe that the Liberal Studies staff cared about them. To make things worse, I was prevented from using the TV studio with them for many weeks by another member of staff who claimed that his work with full-time students gave him the right to exclusive booking of the studio at that time. This problem was resolved by a higher College authority and a fair allocation of TV diary slots was allocated.

Now on course for filming, I offered the class the 'courtship' theme of 'the flash guy and the steady', referring in the play to the contrasting fortunes of William (a 'steady' who lost his Audrey to the 'flash' Touchstone and the 'steady' Silvius who gains Phebe because the 'flash' Ganymede turns out to be the disguised woman Rosalind). It seemed that this courtship theme would be relevant to the boys in the class at their age and this turned out to be true, some of them classing themselves as long-suffering 'steadies', others as 'flash'.

Francoise, a first year A level girl volunteered to act in role with them. She was shocked by the rudeness of some of the boys in the first session, but the boys who were polite to her apologised for the behaviour of the others. In the following session the polite boys responded to the suggestions she made for the drama and gradually a change came over the class as the others became interested and contributed ideas. Francoise was amazed at this change of mood which her presence had effected. **As I explained to her, these events demonstrated the effectiveness of a person outside of the group acting in role and in particular of a girl of their age.**

Although all the boys were keen to work the technical equipment and cameras of the TV studio, none were prepared to take part in the acting. I therefore delegated several of the A level boys to do that in the first filmed episode. However the tape-recording of their work failed and they had to go off to another lesson. Francoise acted skilfully. Grabbing the arm of a Greek boy, Andy, and of an English boy, John, she said: "Come on guys. You can do the acting. You've seen how it's done."

Such was her enthusiasm that they could hardly resist and they made the episode. They were very good, Andy's sense of fun inspiring the dialogue as the flash guy winning over Francoise in role as the contested girl.

They set the scene (in the parallel to which Touchstone tries to fake 'marry' Audrey but is prevented from doing so by Jaques) in a registry office. Andy delegated his friends, Costos and Neil to be the false registrar and witness in the office, Costos masquerading as the registrar in return for considerable payment (with excellent Greek bargaining by Andy and Costos over the sum to be paid). This was foiled by the girl Francoise in role who was delighted with the idea of a marriage to Andy, but insisted that a proper witness be brought from outside the room. This was someone who knew the real identity of Costos and insisted that the real registrar perform the ceremony. Francoise innocently interpreted Andy's action as unintentional and teased him for making a mistake, whipping him out of the room and into the registrar's marriage room.

The class so enjoyed making the film of 'the flash guy and the steady' that they decided to make other episodes, adding a variety of scenarios on the theme.[2] This began with an episode set in a pub where Andy and Alan (a 'steady') were playing cards as Andy boasted about his prowess with women. However this boasting was short-lived as he had been married for some years to a very bossy wife. The class decided that I should act in role as the wife but were horrified by my performance in roughly taking Andy out of the pub by the arm: "Do you behave like that with your own husband, Miss?"

As the 'steady', Alan was left in possession of the field and he went off triumphantly with the devastated Francoise. As he had often been uncooperative in class I was pleased with his participation in the filming.

Further variations featured, milking the theme. Sadly Francoise had to leave the College due to financial reasons so the class had to represent her presence. They then cast me as her mother trying to persuade the 'steady' that she really wanted him. However when he returned to the pub he found out that she was apparently having an affair with his best friend, Alan. He found another girl (my A level student Sally, who had joined us for the class) and they "walked away into the sunset" as he put it. I was pleased with this conclusion, hoping to end the 'courtship' scenarios with triumph for the 'steady' to reassure those in that category in the class!

I decided that the class needed a greater extension of their creativity beyond the variations on 'the flash guy and the steady' theme. The Greek boys were becoming increasingly interested in the acting and liked the mafia style of the *As You Like It* kind of events as I related them in terms of the conflict between brothers in a gang, the younger winning a fight against a tried fighter. In the version of the story as I told it, the gang leader's niece falls in love with the victorious younger brother but is sent away as the gang leader dislikes her. His daughter accompanies the niece and they meet the younger brother in a faraway place. The older brother is also sent away by the gang leader, he falls in love with the gang leader's daughter and there is a double wedding.

The class set this filmed series in an articulated lorry business, the younger brother, Neil, objecting to the older brother (Andy) refusing to allow him to draw money from the firm's takings. Andy arranged for Neil to fight Costos but Neil, thinking that he had killed Costos, escaped to South America with George's sister who was fed up with George. George summoned Andy who demanded that he bring back Neil who owed him money and repatriate his sister. In South America Andy found himself in trouble in a casino but was rescued by Neil who took him back to his apartment where he met George's sister (my A level student Lesley).

They concluded this scenario happily. Neil won enough money gambling to pay back George who wrote to him that Costos had not died but recovered so that Neil could return to the UK. At the wedding of Andy and George's sister and Neil and her friend (another A level drama student) Costos and George, in the spirit of reconciliation, became their best men at the ceremony.

The attitudes and behaviour of the class in this very complex well-acted series represented a complete turnaround from the disgruntled group of boys that I met during my first lesson with them, a tribute to Dorothy Heathcote's system of drama-in-education, the College TV studio and the girls acting in role.

However that was not the only benefit of the filming. Andy who had taken the leading role in most of the filming and who had become deeply interested in acting, was able, with others in the class, to visit the Theatre Set-Up performance of *As You Like It* at Forty Hall, Enfield. He was ecstatic about it, wanted to see the play every night and to go to different kinds of theatre. It was as if a new world had been opened up to him. He came by himself to see the Theatre Set-Up performance of *The Tempest* at Forty Hall in 1982. When I told the Head of the Liberal Studies Department about this he commented, "Sometimes it is only one swallow that does make a summer!"

I learnt from this that I should not be discouraged if at first a class seems uncooperative in drama-in-education as there may be someone in the class whose latent interest may be stimulated by the class work into a new appreciation of another aspect of living.

Fig. 12 *The Flash Guy and the Steady*, Touchstone and William court Audrey (*As You Like It*, V. i.) Tresco Abbey Gardens

Fig. 13 *The Ideal Society*, In the Forest of Arden (*As You Like It*, II. vii.) Lyme Hall

CHAPTER FIVE

As You Like It: class MVM 2D

CLASS MVM 2D

The work of Class MVM 2D was remarkable, producing many innovative ideas.

This class contained a number of boys who had been in the class of the previous year, MVM 1A.

The A level Drama student, Sally, who had worked with them the previous year was not able to attend their lectures at the time they were held (first lesson Monday morning) but Lorraine who had acted in role as a girl disguised as a motor vehicle mechanic apprentice (analogous to Viola's male disguise in *Twelfth Night*) with MVM 1E in 1978–79 was able to be present. This was most fortunate as Lorraine had become expert, not only at acting in role but at dealing with the motor vehicle mechanic apprentices. She and I had decided that this time she would be in role as Rosalind but we knew that we could not repeat the role of girl dressed as boy as the class had seen the film made of her by MVM 1E and would not tolerate the repetition of that theme as it would appear to be copying. We would call the theme 'disguise'.

The sessions did not begin well. Lorraine and a first year Drama student (who later was not able to come to the class) entered the room with me. The boys were surprised. There were insufficient chairs for everyone, including the girls, to have a seat. I asked that some boys give up chairs for the girls who were our guests and find some other chairs from an adjacent room. There was no response. I said that if my request was not complied with the girls would leave. There were rumblings of protest, but after a few moments one boy went out of the room and came back with chairs. After that there was always respect for the girls.

We all discussed what form the theme of 'disguise' should take. I had decided that the learning area be concerned with rebel organisations. I chose this as it was topical in the news and these boys, being second years, were at a fairly rebellious stage. Members of staff always found the second year classes difficult as they had neither the young liveliness of the first years or the increased maturity of the third and fourth years. If the 'disguise' theme could command their respect, they might work out some of their rebelliousness through it and we might move to a good working relationship together. This turned out to be an accurate assessment of the situation and the plan worked.

It appeared that there was an interest in drug-taking in the class so discussions revolved around that during the first planning session during which the class was unruly and unwilling to cooperate. After the lesson the girls and I were walking along the corridor when David, one of the boys from the class passed us. I knew from the previous year that he was a quiet and intelligent member of the class, so we asked his opinion of what we should do with the class. He said that he was interested in drug-taking and that the rebel organisation could be an organisation for the production of cannabis. He continued to talk rationally to the girls and they were amazed as their impression of the class intelligence, gleaned from the previous lesson, had not been high.

In the next session, David, his friends in the class and the two girls then managed to gain control over the class and the whole mood of the class changed permanently. Their enthusiasm for the subject was sufficient to carry the others with them. They decided that David's idea of an organisation designed for the production of cannabis was good. Jenny could be in role as David's girlfriend while Lorraine would be the disguised one, a policewoman infiltrating the group.

Discussion centred on drug-taking and the things the organisation would need to do. Another boy, Iain, emerged in the discussions as a very rational being. He was unlike any other MVM that I had taught, being a well-read (and incidentally mentally frustrated) person. He had read the plays of Shakespeare. At the time both he and David were taking 'soft' drugs. It was decided that David would be the president of the organisation and Iain the secretary.

Detailed preparation for the first episode was made in which they formulated items for the constitution of their organisation which they called 'The Society for Greater Personal Liberty'. Emphasis was placed on their wish for cannabis-taking to be a civil, not criminal offence, symbolising a greater personal freedom of behaviour within society. Procedures for growing cannabis were detailed. Correct committee procedures were discussed and the decision was taken to exclude all but the present members from the organisation. However they decided to have a celebration party with a barmaid from outside serving. Lorraine, the policewoman (with the false name of Marilyn) was to infiltrate the group as the barmaid, oust Jenny in David's affections and replace her on the committee. Iain was to object to Lorraine's presence and oppose her constantly. This episode was satisfactorily filmed.

Jenny was subsequently unable to come to the class so they decided that she and David would have quarrelled and parted. The party episode was filmed in the TV studio but as David found it embarrassing trying to court Lorraine and she was correspondingly embarrassed, the filming did not go well.

During the week Lorraine and I discussed the session fully. She said that she was going to get to know the boys out of class time. She claimed that the socialising in the college refectory with the previous class, MVM 1E, with whom she had worked during the previous year had been the factor that had helped her work with them so successfully in class.

I explained to her that at the moment the sessions posed a moral problem. The law of the country stated that teachers should inculcate good morals in the students and that conclusions to invented stories should, if possible, be morally correct (a situation to be compared with the moral endings of Shakespeare's own plays perhaps suggesting that he might have been in a similar position). We were therefore morally obliged to resolve the drug-taking story in such a way that both David and Iain stop taking drugs. It would be quite good if that happened in real life as well. Lorraine decided that a possible ending for the film would be for David and her to fall in love and marry. Thus she could not testify against her husband in court. We were given another clue to a solution to the problem by an incident that had occurred during the filming. I had said to David: "Come on, take notice of Lorraine."

He had replied: "I can't while I'm smoking."

We thought that David could be presented with a choice – Lorraine or drugs.

The situation became ironical as Lorraine began to go out with David and he gave up drug-taking to please her! I learnt this on the occasion when we broached the subject to David of having to choose in the film between Lorraine and drugs and he was more amenable to it than I had thought he would be. This, I later realised was because the situation had become real![1]

In the episode where the close relationship between Lorraine and David was to be manifest, Iain, upon discovering this, would be told by David that he intended to resign from the group. I decided to press for David to lose his embarrassment in the filmed scenes with Lorraine so began the episode with a long kiss between Lorraine and David. This experiment evidently succeeded as he was not embarrassed and, in fact, spoke quite analytically afterwards to the lecturer, Les, who had the class for the following period. This was the first time that we had ever been able to do an intimate scene in the studio. It marked for me an advance in the power the studio had over the students.

Most of the boys in the class wanted to kill off David in the next episode! He claimed that their motive was jealousy of his relationship with Lorraine (which I thought was the truth) but they gave a variety of reasons why the gang members could no longer trust David as he had collaborated with a policewoman and abandoned them. They also claimed that a murder would "liven things up".

They filmed this episode with great gusto. David acted being tricked into being stabbed by several of the gang members (Lorraine giving much drama-lesson-informed instruction on how to dramatically kill and be killed). The class had decided that one of the boys would have fallen asleep due to an overdose of drugs so that when the police arrived, he was arrested for the murder, the real culprits having escaped. The boys were very pleased with this conclusion to the series but I wondered if I had done wrong in allowing them this immoral ending in the interests of observing their creative freedom, rather than guiding the series to a moral ending. My sole comfort was that the series had succeeded, although through the intervention of true romance, in getting both Iain and David off drugs in real life!

After much debate the class then decided to film a series about the theme 'The Ideal Society' (as in the Forest of Arden community in *As You Like It*). **This 'Ideal Society' would represent what the boys themselves wanted. This series, not set by them in the garages, pubs or clubs that featured in many of the classes' films, but in the realms of their own real-life aspirations, produced the most fruitful in terms of creative learning of all the films made by the motor vehicle mechanics, some of the ideas that they suggested in the episodes (such as having a social worker and a tribunal allocated to every district to solve conflicts) proving so sensible that were they to be adopted by real societies, many social problems within them would be resolved.**

It was at this time that I came to know the extraordinary circumstances of the student Iain. As well as having read the plays of Shakespeare he wrote poetry. He complained that he found few people to talk to in his job. When I asked him why he had not gone to university as his mates had done, he replied that he did not think that university had the answers for him. I realised that I had to find material in the classwork to give him the intellectual 'stretching' that he needed. He expressed a wish to act in role as Lorraine had done. We decided that he would act in role as a newcomer to the 'Ideal Society' that the class devised, and that generally he would hold points of view opposite to those of the Society. He took that kind of role so that, should the occasion demand it, he could provoke argument and response from the others and create tensions which would put the society to the test. He emphasised to me that he did not himself share the points of view of the person he was playing.

The details of the 'Ideal Society' were finalised by the class:

a – There would be capital punishment, in fact hanging, for murder and terrorism but no punishment for other crimes.
b – There would be no marriage.
c – If people wanted to have a committed relationship, they could, but generally men and women would live apart.
d – Any children would remain with the mother, but the boys demanded that the fathers have access to the children.
e – The Society would pay for the maintenance of all children.

f – Those who wished to live apart from everyone else had the freedom to do so.
g – If two men wanted the same woman she would have the freedom to choose, either to have one of them or both.
h – Men would have the same choice if wanted by several women.

In the initial episode Iain in role was introduced to the 'Ideal Society' and after its tenets were explained to him he decided to stay. However in following episodes he challenged the Society's lack of justice in not punishing crimes other than murder and terrorism and he became possessive over a woman.

By now I had decided that this series provided good practical learning material concerned with crime, justice, punishment and relationships within a family. At some point a woman had to object to the imposition of total responsibility for looking after the children. The boys considered that all women must be pleased to have their children omnipresent. This is not necessarily so and the boys had to learn this. When I consulted the married women among the TOPS students, they insisted that this learning be implemented.

We were able to do this in the conflict between a male parent (played by Colin) and his 'wife' over the care of their children. A student teacher, Corrine, had agreed to act in role and when I informed Colin that I was bringing in his 'wife', he was so absorbed in his role that he expressed a delight in the realisation of her as his 'wife' which he maintained in role when she came into the class. The dilemma faced by this couple in the story was that the 'wife' had become pregnant and wanted an abortion as she did not wish to face any childcare duties in addition to those she had at present with two other children. She demanded that if Colin wanted the child he should parent it, a suggestion that he refused to accept.

There was a strong sense in the class of complete protection of children who were valued above all other aspects of the Society. Abortion was therefore prohibited. The class discussed all kinds of possible solutions to the problems which could arise when parents faced conflict between following a career and parenting. It was proposed that a crèche should be established and the boy Clyde volunteered to look after the children placed in it. This I found interesting as it seemed to expose a deep-down wish to live a life other than that he had at the time – in which he worked full-time during the day and did extra work repairing cars during the evenings and weekends.

During the class discussion of Colin and Corrine's argument, Colin insisted that Corrine have the baby and David suggested that the solution might be to put it full-time in a crèche.

"Why should I go through the whole nine months of pregnancy in order just to place the child in a crèche?" countered Corrine.

"Put it to a committee," suggested Ali.

So then the class decided on the brilliant device of having a committee (or a tribunal) to decide on all the problems that might arise within a community. Each district would have a tribunal to whom any person in that society could appeal for arbitration if there were disputes between members. This also applied to any social problems which might occur. The problem of a possible male bias in this tribunal was discussed and the possibility that Corrine would reject any decisions taken by an exclusively male group. That decisions should be taken not necessarily by men or women but by 'people' was discussed, but in order to correct any gender imbalance the class decided that I was to be in role as part of the tribunal with Ali. They also decided that each district would have a social worker and delegated the student Mick to perform that role in the filming.

I expected that this would be one of the most exciting filming sessions in terms of the content of the debate that we had ever made in the TV studio with the mechanics students and so it turned out to be. Corrine and I were in role, she presenting the 'feminist' point of view and I as the chairperson of the tribunal, supporting the values that the class had chosen.

There were two scenes. The first presented the arguments between Corrine and Colin over who would look after their third child and whether it should be aborted, with Mick as the mediating social worker. This scene I pre-planned and set, but when it took place they improvised much dialogue around new ideas that occurred to them on the spot. So important was the sequence of ideas for both this and the next scene that I had them filmed without rehearsal, ignoring technical faults, so that the ideas should be freshly captured on film.

The second scene was the tribunal trial, Mick presenting the case of Corrine and Colin to Ali and myself. Ali was nervous, not knowing what to say. I told him to apply direct judgement and to decide himself what should be done. This he did most competently and presented the couple with the possible solution, that Colin should look after one of the present children, a young boy, thus lightening the burden of Corinne's duties. **Colin, absorbed in his role, seemed to light up at this suggestion, agreeing enthusiastically to look after his imaginary young son. It was one of the loveliest moments in all of the motor vehicle mechanics' filming.**

Corrine in role still pressed for an abortion, claiming that the pregnancy was unplanned due to the failure of the Society's contraceptives. The tribunal apologised for that and promised that she would be given every assistance, medical and domestic in her bearing of the child. Mick, the social worker, would ensure that both the Society and Colin would carry out their promise. She was firmly denied the right to an abortion as her child was precious to the Society and if she wished to remain in the Society she would have to obey its rules. The boys had been unanimous in their protective attitude towards children, which I wished to reinforce, while at the same time trying to introduce concepts of greater understanding and consideration towards women and mothers.

The next precept of the 'Ideal Society' that needed to be challenged was the lack of punishment for any crimes except murder and terrorism. The class decided that Iain would protest to the tribunal about the non-punishment of a man (played by Steve) for his having badly beaten up a homosexual (played by Richard). Motives for violence and toleration of homosexuality were debated. Steve claimed that he would have beaten up Richard "just for kicks". The issue, 'Is it possible for people to be unmotivated in their violence?' was debated by the class. I was concerned to find that the majority opinion favoured unmotivated violence which they considered to be necessary in society for its own sake. Someone suggested that Steve would have attacked Richard for his having "made a homosexual attack" on him. I seized on this as it would not only provide a motive for Steve's violence but would test the class's attitude towards toleration of homosexuality. The class vote on that issue showed a predominance of intolerance.

The above-planned episode was filmed. All the issues we had decided to explore were remembered and brought before the tribunal by Iain. It was upon Ali's skill as a counsellor of social problems that I was focusing my attention. It was he who had solved the previous problem taken to the tribunal and in this filming session he again proved his ability in this field. As I was in role in the tribunal supporting the attitudes of the class I took no original decisions myself, only summarising and clarifying issues as they arose (in Dorothy's system, the teacher facilitator). If a value judgement had to be made I turned towards Ali so that he was encouraged to give the answer. He conceived a very fair solution to the problem, one that could reasonably provide a model for such cases in our own society. In reparation for what had been done to Richard (the class had decided that he had severely damaged his brain), Ali suggested that Steve be made to give up his present job as an engineer and devote his time to inventing and repairing life-support machines in the hospital to which Richard was now committed for life. Lorraine who was in role as the social worker for the district where Steve and Richard were supposed to live was to supervise Steve's carrying out of the tribunal's decision.

In the second scene Iain and Lorraine in role were alone after the trial. He told her that he was going to leave the Society and he asked her to go with him. Their discussions provoked an interesting issue regarding the ethics of how one's life should be lived. Skilfully posing in role opposite points of view, Lorraine claimed that David would be very unhappy if she left and that she now had a new responsibility to Steve and Richard. Iain countered that a person should think only of their own good, not that of society's.

In the next series to be discussed and filmed the class combined the topics of the first two themes, 'disguise' and 'The Ideal Society', the orientation however being within the sphere of politics. I was seeking to monitor the political ideals of the class and to perhaps stimulate them to a degree of thought about political ideals. An interesting fact emerged however with the opinions of the two black boys in the class, Joe and Peter, who held harsher views on democracy than the rest of the class. They considered that an ideal political leadership in a country would be a benevolent dictatorship which sacrifices the freedom of the individual to the welfare, especially the economic

Fig. 14 *Disguise,* Rosalind with Orlando and Celia (*As You Like It*, III. iii.) Forty Hall

welfare, of the country as a whole.

The series, which they called 'The King', was to consist less of the debates that had typified their previous series and more of action and plot. The political ideals of the class would be reflected in the speech made after his coronation by the King.

In the story that the class decided upon, within an African country a king and his party (played by Joe, Ali and Peter) have gone into hiding, taking up a disguise of workers in a restaurant. They have hired a group of English mercenaries to assist them in a military coup which will place the King on the throne, a move approved by the people of the country who have asked for the return of the King in a national referendum. David, the leader of these mercenaries was to be approached by Iain (one of a group of terrorists who did not want the return of the monarchy) who asked to be able to kill the King when he is found. However Iain (who was to oppose the manifesto of the King and his party) and his terrorists were to be killed and in his coronation speech the King would reaffirm the political ideals of his party (and of the class). I supported the story's triumph of the King above Iain's terrorists after the ideals of the 'Ideal Society' of the previous series had been discarded by him. I considered it important that the class should not feel that idealism is always quashed.

Following scenes were filmed in which the King, disguised as a waiter was able to spy upon Iain and David discussing Iain's proposal of betraying the King in a restaurant and another in an office where hard bargaining on the subject took place, revealing the student-participants' skills as hard-headed business men.

The class decided that Iain's killing should be represented, thus avoiding technical difficulties. David and Mick, representing in role the mercenaries, would be handed over their earned fee and Joe would reveal his identity to an astonished David. At that time Joe's bearing was not king-like but we planned that this should be changed by his wearing appropriate costume in an outside environment. In order for him to have faith in his ability to be a king in the filming, he needed to see himself on film in the mode of a king.

With this in mind I planned the last episode in this series, the coronation. I wanted to create a double link of their story with the Theatre Set-Up performance of *As You Like It* by filming a celebration (such as ends the play) in the gardens of Forty Hall, Enfield where at least some of the class would see the performance of the play. The celebration would be the coronation of Joe as King. Arrangements were made for the class to do their filming at this location in class time, going in the college minibus, with the TV studio lecturer filming with the outdoor camera.

This was definitely Joe's day of triumph. Until this series he had not figured at all in the filming but on that day he rose above his peers, not only in his willingness to rise above their possible scorn by wearing a fancy foreign costume (half African but with an Indonesian headdress) but he was willing to pose before a blossom tree in the garden of Forty Hall for his speech. (Such a background would normally be considered a bit effeminate by these boys.) **In his speaking of the King's coronation speech he achieved a dignity akin to majesty.** I was glad that he was one of those that came to see the performance of *As You Like It* at Forty Hall.[2]

A number of boys in the class were able to see the play at Forty Hall, recognising themes in it filmed by them and other classes and enjoying and understanding the text. Sadly neither David nor Iain were among that group as at the time they were abroad on holiday!

CHAPTER SIX

The Tempest (academic year 1981–82); Summerfield Centre (2000–01); Reflections on the work with mechanics students and young people excluded from school

This chapter compares the sessions applying the Dorothy Heathcote principles (but not directly guided by her) to workshops given to young people excluded from school at the Summerfield Centre with the sessions given to the motor vehicle apprentices whose work she supervised at Southgate College.

THE TEMPEST (1981–82)

Encouraged by the work done with the mechanics from 1978 to 1980, from 1981 to 1982 I continued working with mechanics classes at Southgate College on themes from Shakespeare's *The Tempest*, treated metaphorically as in *Twelfth Night* and *As You Like It*. Girls from the A level Drama class continued to work in role with the boys, some of them becoming so expert in the techniques that we employed, that in their following professional lives they used the Dorothy Heathcote strategies in theatre-in-education programmes and drama teaching.

The boys continued to find the same solutions to the conflicts and problems in the stories arising from the themes from the plays that Shakespeare did. I was most pleased with their solution to the theme in *The Tempest* of 'what would you do if all your enemies fell into your hands? Cynics of the nature of the mechanics classes might have imagined all kinds of violent resolutions to this situation, but the boys, even without access to the kind of magic that Prospero's Ariel could supply, chose Shakespeare's course of action: "We are going to try to reform them, Miss, and make them better people so that they become our friends."

As in the previous years, the mechanics students came to see performances of *The Tempest* presented by Theatre Set-Up at Forty Hall, Enfield, understanding and enjoying it.

SUMMERFIELD CENTRE (2000–01)

In 1999 I was at last able to try out the filmed drama-in-education work pioneered with the Southgate College mechanics with young people who had been excluded from school and who were provided with a substitute education (including studying for GCSE examinations) at the Summerfield Centre, Leyton Green Road, London E10. There were facilities for filming, done by a staff technician with a Sony Rover camera in the Centre itself and a technician-staffed TV studio available for all the schools in the borough, some distance from the Centre. I was employed to take a one-and-a-half-hour session with the pupils on Wednesday afternoons.

The main problem for me was that it was the principle of the Centre to do drama-in-education and filming work only with items from current affairs. The source of what I considered to be so many universals applicable to the experience of the pupils in plays by Shakespeare was strictly forbidden! As a result of this I found that the material, sourced from press reports, did not engage the pupils as much as had the Shakespearean themes. The available TV studio did not offer the pupils the several professional-looking cameras like the Southgate College studio ones so there was not the attraction to the pupils of their participation in the actual filming, all of this being done by the staff technician. The technical filming in the Southgate TV studio was often the hook that lured the students into the dramas. The studio was also a considerable travelling distance from the Centre which put some pupils off making the journey.

The pupils were mixed, with behavioural problems which, quite frankly, were less negative than those I had experienced among some of the Southgate College mechanics. A class consisted of no more than six with a predominance of boys over girls. In both years the sessions began with filming of current affairs events with a group of four to six pupils, but then tapered off to continuous sessions with just one pupil who had become fully engaged with the dramas and on whose educational needs I was able to completely focus. It was to the considerable credit of the Centre that they supported the expense of the work being done to the advantage of just one pupil. They considered it worthwhile if it advanced that pupil's learning and their involvement in an educational enterprise.

In the first year while I was working with just one pupil, it became possible to again use a teenage girl working in role. I had done supply teaching in a secondary school where two of the drama pupils were looking for opportunities to do their work-experience and I offered them to work alongside me with the theatre company and in role in Summerfield Centre. The result of the girl's participation in the lesson on the boy in the class was miraculous. He and the girl were able to relate to each other in terms of the music they enjoyed and the clubs that they went to. In role she involved him in the drama we were working on so effectively that even without her subsequent presence, he enjoyed the following sessions and did good filming work where his learning developed and his social confidence increased.

By then my increased age made me appear to the pupils as being in the same generation as their mothers and I exploited this, always expressing a kind of maternal concern on their health and safety. For example if they swung on the overhead bars in the TV studio I did not reprimand them for possibly damaging the bars but expressed concern that they might hurt themselves. They responded well to this.

I sometimes went into role as a mother in their scenarios. In the last sessions of the second year this produced very good work from the boy who had become the one for whom the sessions were being run. The current world event which was the subject of the episodes we were filming was a serious volcanic eruption in a far-off country.

I was having treatment at the time for skin cancer and my face was very scarred from this so we pretended that I had been burnt from the volcano and it was the job of the pupil (who had adopted the character of a social worker) to try to rehabilitate me, as in role I was too scared to go outside my home again and unwilling for my scarred face to be seen. His invention was miraculous as he tried many devices to get me outside my house. Finally he found one that worked: "I shall bring the luxurious Mercedes Benz saloon car of my friend to take you to and from the shop where we can buy you new clothes to replace those that were burnt. We can also get you make-up there to cover your burns."

Who could resist such a suggestion? So we imagined that the scarred and fearful woman that I was playing would leave her house again and be comforted by luxury, new outfits and a repaired face. It was a good end to the sessions![1]

REFLECTIONS ON THE WORK WITH MECHANICS STUDENTS AND YOUNG PEOPLE EXCLUDED FROM SCHOOL

The Mechanics

1 – The mechanics were successful in interpreting themes from the Shakespearean plays, giving them dramatic shape and performing and filming them. A number of them saw the plays presented by Theatre Set-Up at Forty Hall, Enfield, understood them and enjoyed them.

2 – Training took place in:
   a – Memory (needed to accurately remember and reproduce the scenarios).
   b – Imagination (in the interpretation of the themes and the invention of the scenarios).

    c – Language development (by increasing vocabulary and fluency of speech).
    d – Problem-solving (in resolving the problems provoked by the theme or simulated by people in role).
    e – Social and work cooperation (necessary in order to successfully make the films).
    f – Techniques of acting, filming and television studio operation.

3 – **Education took place in these areas:**
    a – Society, its structure and attitudes.
- The proper role of women in society and work (MVM 1E p.33).
- The proper attitude of men to women in society and work (MVM 1E p.33).
- The correct social behaviour in certain circumstances (as courtesy to women and table etiquette) (MVM 1E p.35).
- Accepting women on equal terms at work (MVM 1C p.38).
- The correct behaviour of management and customers in restaurants (MVM 1A p.47).
- Procedure at a tribunal (MVM 2D p.79).
- Toleration of newcomers to a system (MVM 1E p.55).
- Benefits which are brought to a system by newcomers (MVM 1E p.55).
- Hobbies and their accessibility (MVM 1E p.55).
- Prejudice against people because of their appearance (MVM 1E p.57).
- The ethics of drug-taking (MVM 2D p.74).
- An 'ideal society' in these aspects: marriage, the care of children, crime and punishment (MVM 2D pp.77–81).
- The ethics of abortion (MVM 2D p.78).
- Ways in which society could care more for its members: pay for all maintenance of children, supply adequate crèches for children of working parents, provide social workers to whom all social and family problems could be taken and tribunals which could fairly arbitrate between conflicting members of society; men and women to have equal rights and children be highly valued (MVM 2D pp.77–84).
- Aspects of courtship: exploiting and being exploited by

members of the opposite sex, the ethics of being faithful to a partner, the relative success of different modes of courtship (MVM 3C pp.67–69).
- Crime and attendant fear and recrimination; the consequences that can come from even slight involvement with criminals (MVM 3C p.69).
- Language appropriate to different occasions (MVM 2D p.73).

b – Politics.
- The possibility of a government's deeper involvement with social problems within a family and with child care (MVM 2D pp.78–79).
- The variety of possible political systems that can be applied to the running of a country (MVM 2D p.79).
- What political systems might be applied to an emerging nation (MVM 2D p.80).
- Monarchy – advantages and disadvantages; the ideal style of a monarchy (MVM 2D p.83).
- What would be the policies of a benevolent monarch (MVM 2D p.83).

c – Human relationships and behaviour.
- The nature of exploitation and gullibility (MVM 1C p.40, MVM 3C p.64).
- 'Pride comes before a fall' (MVM 1E p.55).
- The relationships between those who live together, especially those who have children (MVM 2D pp.78–81).
- The relationships within families – siblings, power struggles within a family, the loyalty of family members towards each other if threatened from outside the family (MVM 3C p.69).
- Leadership and the importance that being trusted has upon the leader (MCC 2A p.61).
- Hypocrisy – the danger of people trying to pretend to be what they are not or to understand procedures with which they are unfamiliar (MCC 2A p.64).

d – Business.
- The proper way to administer a cooperative enterprise (MVM 2D p.75).
- The correct way to run a committee (MVM 2D p.75).
- How to formulate the constitution of an organisation (MVM 2D p.75).
- The fair delegation of responsibilities in a small business (MCC 2A p.62, MVM 3C p.69).
- The possible value of competition in business (MCC 2A p.62).
- The possible advantages of the association or amalgamation of small firms to survive against competition from larger firms (MCC 2A p.62).

e – The relationship between management and employees in industry.
- Victimisation of employees in industry and how to combat it (MVM 1C p.40).
- The proper rights of employees in industry, industrial strikes, their operation and possible consequences (MVM 1A p.46).
- Racial prejudice in industry, with consequent victimisation of employees and how to combat it (MVM 1E p.46).
- Giving proper support to fellow employees when they are victimised (MVM 1E p.46).
- The power employees can exert over unfair employers in industry (MVM 1E p.46).
- Mutual toleration in a work situation (MCC 2A p.62).

f – The human condition.
- Being exploitable (MVM 1C p.40, MVM 3C p.67).
- Maintenance of integrity against pressure (MVM 1C pp.41–42).
- Problems of identity (MVM 1A p.46).
- Being different from others (MCC 2A pp.61–62).
- The dangers of disguising who you are (MVM 1E pp.36–37, MVM 2D p.76, MCC 2A p.63).
- Naivety (MCC 2A p.64).

Attempts to change any negative behaviour or attitudes of the mechanics by the use of the drama-in-education process

1 – The problem embedded within the story is given an ethical resolution (MVM 1E pp.37–38).
2 – The mechanics are brought to terms with real, not glamorised or idealised, situations. MVM 1E (p.54) where several characters suffer from 'the takeover'; MVM 2D (pp.78–79) were made to face the real problems that their idealised society had created; MVM 3C (p.68) where the 'steady' does not always win the girl he is courting yet the 'flash' guy can meet with trouble.
3 – They are made to explore different aspects of a phenomenon, its advantages and disadvantages (MVM 1E p.54).
4 – They are educated in possible or acceptable procedures within situations which they might experience (MVM 1C p.38, MVM 2D p.73).
5 – In their response to the girls acting in role in the class with them, their behaviour is modelled (as Lorraine and Jane provided MVM 1E (p.54) with a real test of their attitude to women).
6 – Sometimes, in order to promote learning, a taboo subject, such as drug-taking, is made the subject of the drama and its ethics explored (MVM 2D pp.74–76).
7 – Ethical solutions to problems within the drama are posed by people in character (as Ali suggested reparation as punishment, MVM 2D p.81).
8 – Unrealised aspects of a problem are exposed by people in role (as did Corrine in MVM 2D p.80).

Main conclusions

1 – A great number of mechanics have inherent interpretative, imaginative and acting ability which they are willing to put into practice if given the opportunity.
2 – There is no connection between social class and the performance of, or understanding and appreciation of drama.

3 – A television studio in a college can provide incentive for people to make filmed dramas within which they may explore learning.
4 – Dramatic processes, especially if filmed, can involve students, especially mechanics students, in learning which they are often unprepared to explore in oral discussion or the written word.
5 – Girls of the same age as the mechanics students can have a great influence on them in role.
6 – Themes taken from Shakespeare's plays provide excellent material for drama-in-education classes with mechanics.

Summerfield Centre

1 – Young people excluded from school can cooperate with staff and with each other in filming drama-in-education projects.
2 – Themes from Shakespeare's plays might benefit them better than the subject material for filming being taken from current events which are often finite and fixed, not allowing the pupils sufficient scope for their interpretive imagination.
3 – Girls of their own age are excellent at working with them in role to promote learning.
4 – Drama-in-education filming with individual students can benefit them, clearing personal problems, stimulating them to solve problems and giving them self-confidence.
5 – It is important that the TV studios in which they film have equipment which they can work themselves, providing a hook for the process.

CHAPTER SEVEN

Spin-off; Oral work with secretarial students (academic year 1978–80); Conclusions

This chapter records the inspiration that Dorothy's ideas and methods gave to classes in other sections of Southgate College that she did not actually supervise. Her interest in the relation of Polti's statements of universal themes to her wish that education curricula should focus on universals of human life gave the A level and evening class students excellent material for working on and presenting an evening of interesting performances for all of them. The basis of working metaphorically on themes from Shakespeare's plays gave the secretarial students the means to apply these themes in an interesting way to their prescribed oral exam work, recorded by tape recorder.

SPIN-OFF

Dorothy Heathcote said that she thought that the curriculum for children should be the universals, naming Polti's 36 universals as examples (see above p.20). The A level and evening class students sought to find six of Polti's declared universals in Shakespeare's *As You Like It*, tested against: (a) improvised everyday events, (b) fairy tales, (c) classic Bible stories, and (d) classic Greek myths.[1]

1 – **Revolt**
As You Like It: Orlando revolts against Oliver's base treatment of him (I. 1. 27–84) (see fig. 7).
a – Everyday event: a younger sister confronts her older sibling

over falsely blaming her for breaking crockery.
  b – The fairy tale: Cinderella revolts against her stepmother and stepsisters.
  c – Classic Bible story: Adam and Eve defy God.
  d – Classic Greek myth: Prometheus defies the Gods to give humans fire.

2 – **Hatred of kin**
  As You Like It: Oliver plots with Charles the Wrestler to have Orlando killed (I. i. 120–171).
  a – Everyday event: a sister plans to have something nasty put in the gift of a Mars bar to her hated sibling.
  b – The fairy tale: Hansel and Gretel are cast out by their parents to die in a forest.
  c – Classic Bible story: Lot's wife hates Abraham and his family.
  d – Classic Greek myth: Saturn kills and eats his new-born children in order to prevent them supplanting him, as has been prophesied.

3 – **Daring enterprise**
  As You Like It: Celia and Rosalind decide to leave the court and go to the Forest of Arden (I. iii. 90–134).
  a – Everyday event: three young girls decide to backpack to the Far East.
  b – The fairy tale: Jack and the Beanstalk.
  c – Classic Bible story: David fights Goliath.
  d – Classic Greek myth: Odysseus plans to listen to the sirens.

4 – **Superior and inferior rivalry**
  As You Like It: Touchstone gains Audrey against William's prior claim to her (V. i. 1–59).
  a – Everyday event: at a party one girl wins favour with a particular boy by her superior status and consequent glamorous clothing prevailing over another girl who is poor.
  b – The fairy tale: Sleeping Beauty – who is vanquished by the Queen.

c – Classic Bible story: Jacob and Esau. Clever Jacob wins the duller Esau's birthright with a trick.
  d – Classic Greek myth: The Mount Ida beauty contest: Aphrodite wins the contest over her rivals with a clever scheme – to promise Paris, the judge, the most beautiful woman in the world as his wife.

5 – **Effort to obtain**
  As You Like It: Silvius tries to woo Phebe (III. v. 1–35).
  a – Everyday event: the bank loan. A person of moderate income tries to secure a bank loan.
  b – The fairy tale: the wolf tries to capture and eat the three little pigs.
  c – Classic Bible story: Solomon's judgement. Two women try to possess the same child.
  d – Classic Greek myth: Orpheus tries to get his wife Eurydice out of Hades.

6 – **Enigma**
  As You Like It: Rosalind baffles Orlando, Silvius, and Phebe with a seeming riddle (V. iii. 110–121).
  a – Everyday event: the silver – a husband promises his wife a gift of a precious silver service (a family heirloom kept secretly hitherto in a bank vault).
  b – The fairy tale. Snow White's wicked stepmother deceives her by appearing to be an old woman.
  c – Classic Bible story: Joseph appears before his brothers in Egypt and they do not recognise him.
  d – Classic Greek myth: Zeus disguises himself as a bull in order to seduce Europa.

TWELFTH NIGHT AND *AS YOU LIKE IT* USED AS A SOURCE OF ORAL TEACHING MATERIAL FOR SECRETARIAL STUDENTS IN THE SOUTHGATE TECHNICAL COLLEGE BUSINESS STUDIES DEPARTMENT

Twelfth Night and *As You Like It* proved an excellent source of material for the oral work which I was required to do with seven classes of secretarial students in the Business Studies Department of the College from September 1979 to September 1980. These classes consisted of three kinds: S.T.D.s, women on daytime release from their jobs in industry; CC17 and CC18, girls training for one year to be secretaries; TOPS, women (and sometimes men) training to be audio-typists for six months on the Training Opportunities Scheme (see above p.26). All these students, in addition to receiving training in business and secretarial skills, had to study oral and written English communication, the CC 17 and CC18 classes taking Royal Society of Arts examinations.

The skills required of them in their business oral communication courses are:

1 – That they should be able to speak clearly and fluently, in a style appropriate to business communication.
2 – That they should be able to establish immediate rapport with the person to whom they are speaking.
3 – That they should have the ability to solve the kind of problems with which they could be faced in a business context and to show initiative and quick thinking at all times.

I found that a tape recorder provided the most adequate substitute for the examiner/business associate/employer with whom these students were being trained to communicate and before whom they would need to demonstrate their fluency of speech and ideas. It not only forced them to speak clearly in order that their voices be adequately recorded but gave immediate replay facility so that they could admire or criticise their own work.

The students were already receiving considerable training in the business style of language required of them in this examination through their business studies lectures. It was my task to assist them to be fluent in ideas and speech. To this end I extracted themes from *Twelfth Night* and *As You Like It* which could be interpreted in short improvisations performable by two to four people and spoken into a tape recorder.

The themes from *As You Like It* adapted for use in oral training for the secretarial students:

1 – An argument between two people, one who considers that she is being unjustly treated by the other and not given her owed rights (as Orlando and Oliver, I. 1. 27–75).
2 – An argument between an older sister and an oppressed younger one. A friend tries to mediate (as Orlando, Oliver, Adam, I. 1. 27–79).
3 – Person A warns person B of danger to person C. B organises that the dangerous event should take place (as Charles the Wrestler to Oliver about Orlando, I. 1. 90–110).
4 – A messenger tells of a political takeover, or a business takeover, or a sit-in (as Charles the Wrestler, I. 1. 90–110).
5 – Stupefied reaction (as Orlando to Rosalind's gift after the wrestling match, I. 1. 234–249).
6 – A person's behaviour or attitudes are ridiculed but turn out to be valid (as Jaques is ridiculed for his compassion towards the killed deer and humanity, II. 1. 26–70).
7 – Talk about someone not knowing that person to be present (as Orlando talks of Rosalind throughout Acts III, IV and V).
8 – Try to dissuade someone from entering a competition which you feel that they will lose (as Rosalind and Celia to Orlando, I. 2. 156–180).
9 – In a competition someone boasts that he will win. This spurs on his opponent who defeats him (as Charles the Wrestler to Orlando, I. 1. 187–196).

The women in the classes had great fun with these themes, interpreting them in business, personal and family terms with a resulting confidence in their oral work when they heard their tape-recorded work played back to them. Some of them were surprised that they were working on themes from Shakespeare to whose plays they had been given an unsatisfactory introduction in school.

Examples of their interpretation of theme 6:

1 – Two women are gossiping about the folly of a neighbour who is buying too much sugar. Suddenly a sugar shortage is announced.
2 – Two women are ridiculing a third's wearing of a brightly-coloured dress. She is not involved in a motor accident which occurs to the others because the motorist could not see them in the dark.
3 – Two girls ridicule the man a third is going out with. They say he has no profession but he turns out to be a good motor vehicle mechanic.
4 – A woman is ridiculed for stopping her daughter from enjoying an active social life. Her daughter passes her exams while their daughters (who have been out dancing every night) fail.
5 – Two women ridicule someone for wearing rain-proofed clothes when the sky is so clear. Suddenly the sky clouds over and there is heavy rain.
6 – A girl is ridiculed by two other girls for refusing to eat junk food. However they end up having to go to Weight Watchers.
7 – Two women criticise the person who restricts her daughter from going out. However their daughters get pregnant.

CONCLUSIONS

1 – Shakespeare's plays are sources of universals, which Dorothy Heathcote suggested should be the curricula of schools, demonstrated through at least six of those proposed by Polti and tested by application to stories endemic to UK society.

2 – Shakespeare's plays prove to be a source of material used for oral work in secretarial courses, giving scope for imaginative interpretation.

3 – Dorothy Heathcote's drama-in-education principles of using dramas as learning media are successful in encouraging secretarial students to become confident in speaking publicly into a tape-recorder and subsequently in the business world.

CHAPTER EIGHT

The workshops on *Antony and Cleopatra* and *Much Ado About Nothing* that Dorothy Heathcote took with students of the Mencap National College, Dilston, Northumberland

During the years 1998 and 1999, when these workshops took place, preparing the college students for the public performances of the plays which would take place in the evenings in the college grounds (with the 17th-century chapel as the immediate backdrop), the college was owned and operated by Mencap. Students from the ages of 16 to 25 years were mostly residential, some returning to their home during the weekends. In the extensive college grounds were the ruins of Dilston Castle, making it a heritage site and thus attractive for audiences to the performances of Theatre Set-Up presented there.[1] The students varied in the levels and types of their mental and sometimes physical disabilities, always treated by the staff as the young adults that the college was designed to educate and prepare for life in the world outside the college. Just like other teenagers, some of them were in love with each other, so the themes in the two plays concerning love between protagonists were very relevant to them. For photographs of these workshops, please see www.ts-u.co.uk, 'Special Needs'.

ANTONY AND CLEOPATRA (1998)

This workshop took place in a large marquee situated in the college grounds. All around the edges of the inside of this marquee were tables on which the props and costumes of the production were displayed. The students were invited to enter and look at these by Terry, one of the actors dressed in the costume of the part that he played in the performance. He pointed out that these objects created the world of the play. The students were fascinated by them, and noted how they differed from objects in the real world. For example, the grapes that were used by a courtesan in the play to entice the soldiers to dance in Pompey's on-board party were plastic and the Roman swords were blunt so that they would not hurt the actors using them.

The students were told that they would accompany the actors on a journey through the play. Many of the students had carers with them who helped them throughout the day, acting in role as if, like the students, they were tourists, or pilgrims exploring the world of the play. Dorothy Heathcote would be their guide on this journey and would enter later. The actors acting in and sometimes out of their roles in the play had been given pre-information and were pre-programmed about the themes that could be explored (but were not fixed) on the journey. These were: 'heroes and villains', 'loyalties and taking sides', 'power', 'victims' and 'anti-heroes'. In dealing with these themes, Constantin Stanislavsky's 'Magic If' was to be a big key for the actors and the students. For example the students would be asked, "How would you behave if you were in that situation?" "What if you were the judge of that person?"[2] Terry told the students the main outline of the play-journey they would go on before Dorothy entered as the guide.

After she had entered and addressed the students as their guide on this journey, she introduced the actors who then entered in the costumes of their main roles. She pointed out that they were not really the characters that they were representing in the costumes but actors performing them: "You saw them come in their ordinary clothes to the college in their van didn't you?" she asked the students and some of them said that they had, helping the actors to unpack their gear into the chapel where the props and costumes of the play were to be stored. "When they wear their costumes they become the character that they are going to play, but now they are going to step out of character and explain to you the situation of their character in the play."

Each actor did this, discussing the conflicts their character faced in the story of the play, and Dorothy set out the questions which faced them, such as, "Should Antony go back to Cleopatra or stay in Rome with Octavia?" She then asked the actor performing Antony to give his response to that question within the script of the play, quoting the speech in the first scene of the play which give a sense of the magnitude of his love for Cleopatra:

> "Let Rome in Tiber melt and the wide arch
> Of the ranged empire fall! Here is my space.
> Kingdoms are clay." (I.1. 33–35)

Then scenes were staged episodically, the students, guided by Dorothy, invited to 'drop in' on the action to interrogate the characters, teasing out the themes such as 'loyalty', and possibly to alter the direction of the journey. The students were given the right to change the decisions the characters took, thus creating different outcomes within the play. They could, if they wished, decide that Pompey could be killed at his boat party. Then when they saw the play whose plot held a different outcome from the one they had chosen, they could decide that their solution was a better one! In this way they were wearing the 'Mantle of the Expert' and had ownership of the story. Much attention was given to Antony's decision to return to Cleopatra rather than to stay in Rome where his duty lay. The actor playing Octavius was young, handsome and dressed resplendently. "Why don't you stay with him and with his lovely sister whom you have just married?" they asked. The actors themselves were amazed by how deeply the students became involved with the issues of the play and how emotive their responses were to the play's action. For example they were very concerned for Octavia: "You should have stayed with her!" they exclaimed.

Some students however, thought that Antony was disloyal to Cleopatra in marrying Octavia and reprimanded him sternly for doing so. None approved of him marrying Octavia while loving Cleopatra and then returning to Cleopatra when married to Octavia. The bad treatment of these two women in his life visibly upset them.

Sometimes Dorothy used mime to create a sense of the location of scenes. When a ship or boat scene was forthcoming she held out her hands, inviting all the students to join her in creating the outer shape of the vessel. Then the actors climbed into it and performed the scene. Of great importance was the sea-battle which Antony lost to Octavius because he agreed with Cleopatra to fight by sea with her new ships rather than on land where he fought best: "Why did you do that?" a student asked, appalled by his folly, especially when Cleopatra fled the battle, deserting him.

"Because I love her so much!" Antony replied.

The students were disappointed that Antony's friend, Enobarbus, deserted him. It was such an important issue within the theme of loyalty that Dorothy herself asked him why he did it.

"I don't know. It was a mistake. I was disillusioned with Antony's behaviour as a soldier because he was distracted by Cleopatra," replied the actor performing Enobarbus, his head hanging disconsolately. "I do not want to live anymore." The actor was a very experienced one and his deeply emotional improvised performance at that moment made the students feel very sorry for him.

The outcome of the day's workshop was that different pupils understood the play at different levels. Many might not have grasped it intellectually but they all received it on an emotive level, responding instinctively and spontaneously to the action. It was a very suitable play to explore with the students. Based on the reality of actual historical events with characters who, having actually existed, were plausible and exciting, it provided universal themes concerning the human condition and consequently much valuable life-learning. Dorothy termed such material 'classic' and always promoted it as suitable for children to explore.

MUCH ADO ABOUT NOTHING (1999)

This play was very different, its plot mainly concerned, not with classic but with domestic issues and consequently the workshop had a different impact on the students from the one on *Antony and Cleopatra*. However its core themes on love and marriage were very relevant to the young people, many of them in love themselves or hoping to achieve that happy state. As the key scene in the play features a wedding, the state of love and marriage was explored through the main characters of the story. A group of adult disabled performers called The Lawnmowers whose work was guided by Dorothy assisted for the day. It was very gratifying to the actors who had participated in the *Antony and Cleopatra* workshop that many of the college students recognised them with pleasure when they arrived at the college and they said that they looked forward to working with them again. They were very helpful as before in unpacking the gear from the van into the chapel.

The workshop began with most of the actors costumed in character and out of role outside the marquee with the students and Dorothy. She gave the students the idea that inside the marquee was a special place where important events would take place. This was to give a sense of the church where the play's wedding scene would take place. She also indicated that they were all now in a very lovely place called Messina, in the island of Sicily.

The actor, Terry, costumed and in role as the comic policeman Dogberry was in focus throughout the workshop, leading actions and promoting opinions on the decisions the play's characters made and those proposed by the students. The character he was performing was very attractive to them and as the Master Constable of the men of the Watch whose duty it was to watch over the streets and households of Messina, his role was very appropriate to one of the themes of the play, 'correct observation and listening'. As the students entered the marquee Terry welcomed them as guests to the grand house of Leonato, the Governor of Messina, and told the students that there would be some more guests, soldiers who were returning from a battle which they had won. Accompanying them would be the members of Leonato's family and household.

He then welcomed the actors as they entered, pointing out the different characters that the actors would perform: Leonato, his daughter Hero, his niece, Beatrice, Margaret (a servant), the Prince of Aragon, Don Pedro and his brother Don John with his friends, Borachio and Conrade, and Benedick with his friend Claudio. He explained that some of the actors took several roles for which they would have to change into different costumes, for example that I played Margaret but would change into the costume for Friar Francis. The students then were grouped around different actors who talked out of role to them about their part in the story and the conflicts their acted characters faced. The group around the actor playing Don John, the villain of the piece, learnt that his character was jealous of a young man, Claudio who had won the favour of Don John's brother, Don Pedro. The actor playing Benedick told them that he was at odds with Leonato's niece, Beatrice who liked to make fun of him. The actress playing Beatrice told them that she was having problems with Benedick, who made fun of her! The actor playing Claudio told them that he was in love with Hero but was too shy to tell her or to ask her father for her hand in marriage. The actress playing Hero told them that she rather fancied Claudio. The actor playing Don Pedro told them that he had informed Leonato of Claudio's love for Hero and Leonato had agreed to their marriage.

Dorothy and Terry then supervised the performance of scenes significant to the story, especially the scene (II. 2.) when Don John and his friend Borachio plot to make Hero seem unfaithful to Claudio by getting Margaret to pretend to be Hero leaning out from her bedroom window during the night, as if she were the lover of Borachio who would be talking to her below. The plan was that Don John would get Don Pedro and Claudio to see this at a distance so that they would believe Hero to be a flirt. The students were shocked by this wickedness but wondered if Don Pedro and Claudio would believe that Margaret was Hero. Then they played the scene when Don John tells Don Pedro and Claudio that Hero is flirting with another man and Claudio claims that if this is true, instead of marrying her, "where I should wed, there will I shame her."

As with the *Antony and Cleopatra* workshop, Dorothy made use of Stanislavsky's 'Magic If'. This the students were able to apply to all the scenes, especially the ones concerning the above plot.

"What if the Prince and Claudio went up close to the window and saw that it was Margaret there, not Hero?" The story would then be a happy one as a result of correct observation.

The students were pleased that the Watch overheard Borachio tell Conrade of his betrayal of Hero, and that they arrested the two wrongdoers and took them to Dogberry who went straight away to warn Leonato of what the misinformed Claudio was intending to do. They were alarmed that because Dogberry dithered with his account of the story, Leonato took no notice of it.

"If he had only had the patience to listen to Dogberry, no harm would have come to Hero."

The theme of the kind of listening that occurs when someone overhears other people talking was also then explored in the device their friends invented to get Benedick and Beatrice to believe that they loved one another. This was the kind of observation which had a good result. The students did not want to change the story and were pleased that Beatrice and Benedick might become lovers. However there was another possibility: "What if Beatrice and Benedick guessed that their friends were plotting to match them off to each other and they took no notice?" they speculated.

They were however pleased that that possibility did not occur as Beatrice and Benedick became engaged lovers at the end of the key wedding scene in which Claudio, instead of marrying Hero, accused her of immorality and rejected her. Dorothy made much of the beginning of this scene which she stopped and 'froze' as Claudio looked fiercely at Hero before the friar began the wedding ceremony.

"What do you notice about his expression?" Dorothy asked the students.

"He looks as if he hates her!" exclaimed one of the students.

"I wonder what is the matter? My husband didn't look at me like that on our wedding day. He smiled in a loving way and was happy to see me." Dorothy responded.

The scene was played through and the students were very sorry for Hero who was treated so wrongfully. They engaged deeply with the following story wherein Hero fainted with the shock of Claudio's treachery and Friar Francis suggested that she should pretend to be dead until the situation was resolved. They were pleased to see the honourable nature of Benedick made evident as he judged Hero to be innocent by observing the reactions of Beatrice to the accusations against her cousin.

"Lady Beatrice, have you wept all this while? ... Surely I do believe your fair cousin is wronged."

The students were pleased to note that such was his sympathy for her distress and the wrong done to Hero that he declared his love for her. In return, understanding his sincerity, she responded by declaring her love for him. However they were shocked at what happened next. Beatrice challenged Benedick to prove his love by taking revenge on her behalf on the man who has dishonoured Hero.

"Kill Claudio!" Beatrice commanded.

"Ha, not for the wide world!" Benedick replied.

"You kill me to deny it. Farewell." Beatrice exclaimed.

Now the students had a new problem to discuss. Should Benedick kill his friend Claudio to prove his love to Beatrice? Within the group they took opposing views – some deciding that Claudio deserved it and others claiming that whatever the cause you should never kill a friend.

They then approved the confession of Borachio who sincerely regretted the harm that he had done to Hero, especially as he thought that she had died. This confession resolved the play and Claudio was penitent, agreeing to marry, as compensation for his doing wrong to a woman from Leonato's family without seeing her face at the ceremony. The students queried that.

"Would you marry someone without knowing her, and not even seeing what she looked like?" Most denied that they would. "What if she were some dreadful-looking old person!"

However they were consoled when the unknown bride turned out to be Hero herself, considering it to be a 'lucky chance' and they rejoiced in the happy conclusion of the play with Beatrice and Benedick also planning to marry. They registered that the wicked Don John was a coward, running away from the consequences of his crime, and they were glad that he had been caught and brought back to Messina. With ideas of their own they echoed Benedick's words, "I'll devise brave punishments for him."

The students saw the play that evening with greater insight than they would have had without Dorothy's workshop with them, some of them thinking that the decisions they had made for alternative actions within the plot would also have been interesting. In this sense they had been give the 'Mantle of the Expert'.

CHAPTER NINE

Some of Dorothy Heathcote's life-learning stratagems applied to able-bodied children and to those with special needs

Although I did not consider engaging with special needs pupils in their music lessons through accessing Shakespeare, my confidence had been bolstered by the work with Dorothy Heathcote through him in previous years and I looked to other stratagems in her drama-in-education programmes to enliven music for them.

The **'Mantle of the Expert'** aspect is especially applicable to working with special needs pupils, as the first principle to be followed with them is to give them **the power of control and decision-making** whenever possible. This is because people who are with them often do not have the patience to give them the time to do things for themselves or do not consult them about what they want to be done. Dorothy's principle of **making ideas concrete and always providing props, costumes and even elements of scenery to drama-in-education** is also very important to these students whose experience of the world has often been limited and they enjoy this being extended into realms beyond their knowledge. Sometimes these objects could be used in **'secondary role'**, a stratagem very appropriate for young people who often endow their playthings and objects in their surroundings with imagined life.

The pupils in the classes at Trinity School, Dagenham, where I did music supply teaching over a period of four years, from 1998–2002, had a wide range of disabilities, usually including a degree of learning difficulty. Some of the pupils were not very disabled at all and could be encouraged to try to enter regular state schools, but some were profoundly disabled, often unable to move or talk, mostly communicating through their eyes. These pupils had a dedicated carer looking after them who could be their substitute for doing the things (which the pupil could indicate through head or eye movement) that they wanted to be done. Some of them suffered continual pain and some could not eat, being fed through tubes. They all loved music and I aimed to make this a medium through which, combined with drama-in-education scenarios and techniques, their range of knowledge and experience could be extended. I did not patronise them with simple nursery rhymes but with good classical music to which they gave an emotional response. I also questioned the exam-dictated syllabus that they were presumed to be able to follow, for example to understand terms, which as a practising musician, I did not recognise as important, such as calling the beat in a bar a 'pulse'![1]

Physical disability was the main problem of the pupils at Woodcroft School, Leytonstone, where I occasionally did supply teaching, so a greater range of cognitive learning could sometimes be achieved. For photographs of sessions, please see www.ts-u.co.uk, 'Special Needs'.

MUSIC FOR SPECIAL NEEDS PUPILS
(1998–2003)

There were two types of activity required by this subject which needed to be integrated into the lessons: making music themselves and listening to it. I tried to incorporate these elements into a drama-in-education form of the lessons. One of my retired teacher friends was very interested in the pupils and supplied me with many material objects for the classes to enjoy.

For all the following work I always tape-recorded everything that the pupils did and then played it back to them so that they could gain satisfaction from their music-making.

There were two songs that could be jokingly dramatised which the pupils in all the younger classes loved to sing every week. 'The Hippopotamus Song' by Flanders and Swann was successful with all the classes but especially with those who were profoundly disabled and could not speak properly but could approximate the chorus chant of "Mud, mud", while others continued with "glorious mud". There were usually nine children in a class and I happened to have nine soft toy hippopotamuses which people had given me over the years, so that each child could choose a hippo-character to act in 'secondary role' the story that I would sing in the verse, while they all joined in the chorus. One hippo was the male hippo, one his female love and the others the hippos who all joined in the fun and jumped into the river Shalima (a blue stretch of cloth). What fun we had as they all threw the hippos into the imagined river with a sung "resounding splash"! The hippos 'lived' in a 'hippopotamus case' and it was always an earned privilege for one of the pupils to bring out the 'hippopotamus case' from the music store, take out the hippos and then put them back again 'to sleep' after the song.

The song which the older children loved to sing also was 'The Mouse in Old Amsterdam'. Audience members in The Netherlands where Theatre Set-Up performed for 19 years had given me joke items such as tiny ornamental clogs, real wooden clogs, a small china windmill and a toy mouse (all of which could function in 'secondary role'). They were astonished when I leapt upon these items as ideal for use in this song.

I sang the verse with the story, the pupils turning the windmill's sails and bouncing the toy mouse and the clogs up and down imaginary stairs. There was great scope for hand action in the song – imitating the clip-clop of the mouse going up the stair or gesturing disbelief in the story. The music class was then divided into two parts for the chorus, each singing the words of the first or second character, the first making great play with the clogs-action and the second with exaggerated gestures for "Oh, yeah?"

First character: "I saw a mouse!"
Second character: "Where?"
First: "There on the stair."
Second: "Where on the stair?"
First: "Right there. A little mouse with clogs on."
Second: "Well, I declare!"
First: "Going clip-clippity-clop on the stair."
Second: "Oh, yeah?"

It was often a good idea to end the lesson with one of these fun songs. Some of these children were predestined to have extraordinarily short lives which most teachers considered should be as enjoyable as possible.

Sea shanties (fortunately as music-curriculum-prescribed work songs, they were the only part of the dictated course that I was happy with) benefited from models I had of the sailing ships *Cutty Sark* and *The Endeavour* which could function in 'secondary role'. The class imagined sailing in these and sang the songs that accompanied the different ships' tasks (like working the capstan) all of which they mimed. My retired friend photocopied extracts from books on the conditions on board these ships and the pupils were astonished at the stories of how young people were press-ganged into the navy and forced to climb right to the top of the masts to change the sails. It gave a reality to the songs that we were singing. By chance, I was able to relate that aspect of history to events in the life of my own family.

"Did you ever know anyone who was press-ganged, Miss?" asked one of the pupils.

"Yes, as my aunt, their sister, described the horror of the event to me, my father and his brother were press-ganged into the First World War by officers of the Ministry of Defence who came and took them out of their croft-farm cottages in the Outer Hebrides of Scotland in the early hours of one morning. The local laird, the land owner of the crofts, had told them where the young boys were."

"I would have killed him when I came back from the war, Miss!"

"Oh, those that survived the war (including my father but sadly not my father's brother) did something much more effective than that. The war had told them how to use guns and when they came back they used their guns to threaten the laird off the island. They then joined forces with the Crofters Commission, a powerful group of many thousands of people in Scotland, which got government support to own their own crofts and never be press-ganged again. My father was given a croft but he gave it to his younger brother and migrated to Australia."

The pupils were amazed at my personal involvement in this history which brought the whole reality of one grim aspect of the past to life for them, and I would never have believed when I started the sea-shanties music lessons that they would, led by a pupil's curiosity, reveal such direct life-learning.

The music trolley, full of dozens of small percussion instruments, proved a good way for the pupils to make music for themselves, and these instruments led the path to an entry into exciting learning areas. My friend also gave us toy Australian animals for use in 'secondary role', and we made up stories about these fascinating creatures, using the instruments to describe their actions and the Australian bush environments they lived in, supplemented by relevant pictures. Following the Aboriginal musical tradition of 'click sticks', we used ordinary rulers or stick percussion instruments to beat a rhythmic accompaniment to a tape I had of Aboriginal song-stories. They could follow the song-pattern of this music and sometimes we would imitate it, singing (with the words formed only in our heads while tapping out the rhythm) our own imagined song-stories. I had an Aboriginal bark painting and those who could, made their own Australian pattern and animal pictures in the lesson while we listened to my tapes of Aboriginals playing didgeridoo music. Australian friends had furnished me with ancient traditional stories which Aboriginals told their children, and the Trinity pupils loved these, accompanying them with suitable music made with their percussion instruments and 'click sticks'. The Australian Aboriginal cultures are many thousands of years old and their children's stories have thus stood the test of time, guaranteeing their appeal!

The pupils loved stories about space, so we would pretend to get into our space travel vehicles with accompanying percussive sounds and visit different planets in the solar system, looking at pictures of them and describing what they were made of with different instruments – solid sounds for the rock planets and quivering light sounds for the gas giants. We were sometimes very adventurous, travelling to the moons of Jupiter or Saturn, the music trolley then being challenged to supply us with musical instruments which could describe what we were seeing there!

The pupils also liked being introduced to different countries through music. I had bags into which had been put tapes of music and objects from a selection of countries. The pupils (including the severely disabled ones, through their carers) would select a bag, and we would play the music of that country on our tape recorder while handling the object around the class, and those capable of doing so would locate the country on a world map. If the carers and I knew a song from that country we would sing it for the children before we played the tape music (this rarely occurred as we did not know the songs well enough not to make fools of ourselves).

I was asked to do music classes with the very young pupils and decided upon classic fairy tales, taking care to avoid *Jack the Giant Killer* (too violent) and *Hansel and Gretel* (as some of the pupils had also been rejected by their birth parents). I learnt to exclude *The Three Little Pigs* from classes as the pigs were offensive to Muslim children. A local shop kindly laminated and photocopied to A3 size pictures from my mother's beautiful 1920s fairy-tale book of these stories: *Cinderella*, *Red Riding Hood*, *Jack and the Beanstalk*, *Puss in Boots*, *Dick Whittington*, *Goldilocks and the Three Bears* and *Beauty and the Beast*. All these stories encapsulate learning areas of their own, a fact which some of the pupils were able to identify. Costumes and props came from my mother's 'memory store' and from Theatre Set-Up's costumes and props box and even from joke gifts from the company's audiences (like a huge artificial red rose presented to me after a performance, which became the rose in the story of *Beauty and the Beast*). A professional mask-maker made masks for some of the stories, particularly the ones featuring animals so that those masks featured in 'secondary role'. I chose music composed by Ravel (who had written several orchestral fairy tales) and Eric Coates (who had done the same and whose music written for his young son and for wartime British workers, had the vibrancy that fitted so many of the stories).

In the lessons the pictures were shown to the pupils and then propped up for everyone to see. Then, putting on the costumes and masks, the children took it in turns to play the different characters in the stories which I narrated for them, timed with the selected music as in 'programme music'. The stories with their music were performed several times so that all the children could perform whatever character they wished to play (some very much assisted by their carers). If there were time left over before the end of the lesson, we would play the music again without the narration and we would all clap to it. This all gave them a realistic sense of the stories that music could tell and introduced many of them to classical music.

In 1977 Theatre Set-Up had performed Shakespeare's *A Midsummer Night's Dream* in the style of an Indonesian dance-drama, using costumes, masks, props and some musical instruments which I had brought back from a visit to Java and Bali. Any of these could be regarded in Indonesian dance-dramas as functioning in the **'secondary role'** which was very much a feature of traditional Indonesian culture. For example, the curved dagger, called a *kris*, often stood for a man of high caste and in olden times if he were to marry a woman of a lower caste, his *kris* would be substituted for his person during their wedding ceremony! The puppets, either three dimensional and carved out of wood and called **wayang golek** or flat and carved out of leather, becoming shadows on a screen when lit from behind and called **wayang kulit**, were considered to have real life and were thought to protect those who owned them or performed with them.

There were nine of these masks or costumes which could be used to represent the main characters in the Indian story of Rama and Sita which formed the basis of a simplified Indonesian **Ramayana dance-drama,** and I could see how this could be performed musically by the pupils on the many xylophones the school had as I narrated the story. It was easy to remove certain keys from the xylophones so that the remaining keys formed the pentatonic scale of the Indonesian gamelan orchestras. Whatever was played with the hammers on the xylophones would then sound just like the gamelan music in the Indonesian *Ramayana.* The **costumes, masks and props, functioning as 'secondary role',** were laid around two desks placed long-ways together and the pupils chose which character they would like to represent, sitting at the desks behind the gear of that character. I did not ask them to put on either the costumes or the wooden masks as they would be uncomfortable and would restrict their musical performance on the xylophones which they could play. Instead, as each protagonist was mentioned in the story, the carers held up the mask or costume which stood for that character. As I narrated the story, the pupils representing the different characters mentioned in the story as it unfolded, hammered the keys of the xylophone according to the mood they found in the action. With some pupils of course, the carers did the hammering for the pupils, guided by their directions or supporting their hands to strike the keys with hammers.

It worked very well and when we played back the tape recording of our efforts to perform a 'gamelan *Ramayana*' at Trinity School, it did actually sound very much like the recordings I had taken in Bali of the gamelan performances of the Ubud dance-drama company in the village where I had been staying. When listening to the tape recording, the pupils were very pleased with their efforts on their 'gamelan' instruments, the carers pointing out the music that each pupil had made when the narration mentioned their character's action in the story. The Hindu epics, such as the *Ramayana*, bring with them their own life-learning, as every one of their episodes gives an account of how to behave or how not to behave and promotes the idea that good should, by people's dedicated efforts, ultimately defeat evil. **This creates ethical learning by affective means through the beauty of art**, more effective than that attempted by prescriptive methods. I hoped that some of this learning was received through affective means by the Trinity School pupils as we made our way musically through our *Ramayana*.

There were more musical instruments in the school's music store which I could see could be used in this way, such as steelpans which the children could easily play, giving them an introduction to different kinds of worldwide music. However I left the suggestion for their use to my successor in the Trinity School music room, along with details of the above-recounted musical efforts I had made there, all motivated by the Dorothy Heathcote stratagems for life-learning that had made the music so enjoyable for the pupils and for myself.

OTHER SPECIAL NEEDS SUBJECTS (1998–2003)

Young special needs pupils are usually free of the kinds of inhibitions which inflict other children, so I found that working with them in any kind of play was a great pleasure. As with other pupils, Christmas was a time to celebrate with nativity plays, and regardless of their religion, the pupils in the class I was asked to look after at Christmas one year thrust themselves enthusiastically into as many and as varied versions of the nativity story as they could invent. The boys were not inhibited in playing women's roles either and as the pupils rotated the story many times around the class, the boys were more than happy to play the leading role of Mary. The intrinsic learning material I identified (necessarily avoiding too much religious significance in consideration of the pupils who observed other-than-Christian faiths) was a sense of the story's history and geography, emphasising this through the costumes and props which I found for them, to give reality to the story. The pupils enjoyed the props for gold, frankincense and myrrh being used in 'secondary role' for the Three Wise Men. However, they insisted on playing the shepherds themselves, some of the pupils enjoying performing their sheep!

Trinity School tactfully observed all the main celebrations of the varied religions followed by the pupils and they were all treated with the same respect, with the associated opportunities for the pupils to enjoy stories from them.

It is important to note here the dedication and creativity of so many special needs teachers. At the Christmas concerts for which the pupils had been preparing for many weeks and which were given at the school on afternoons when some parents could attend, the way the performances were presented was so moving that there were not many dry eyes among the adults in the audience, myself included. This creativity of the staff teaching physical education brought about the same result on one occasion in displays of the work prepared with all the classes in the school. For example, the teacher of one class of very physically disabled pupils announced that they had decided to portray 'flying' in their item. This consisted of course of the carers, sometimes singly or with another carer or member of staff lifting the pupils into different flying positions and carrying them through the air with a variety of flying movements. The children involved in this were shrieking with ecstasy at their release from immobility. All these brilliant members of staff are, whether they realise it or not, incorporating in their creative work many of the stratagems that are encapsulated in Dorothy Heathcote's 'Mantle of the Expert'. The pupils enabled to fly through the air had been given the 'mantle' of birds, the 'experts' in flying. I had learnt about the importance to physically disabled children of being enabled to dance, and these teachers certainly followed that principle with all the classes, the children supported in their movement by carers and staff, and thus being given the chance to enjoy the same pleasure of dancing to music as that experienced by physically abled children.

Regardless of the subject I was supposed to be teaching, I continued, in Trinity School and other special needs schools in which I was supply teaching, to always give material substance to ideas, preferably using inanimate objects in 'secondary role' even if that meant making drawings of them. In doing this I was not exceptional, the carers and members of staff making every effort to relate the subject to the lives of their pupils and to draw out life-learning from the subject matter. This need to objectify abstract concepts for children has already been identified in such subjects as arithmetic where songs such as 'There were ten green bottles hanging on the wall...' support the concept of subtraction, and 'One man went to mow...' and 'This old man, he played one...' support addition, with the glee of the mimed chorus, 'Knick, knack paddy-whack, give a dog a bone...' adding the pleasure principle to the learning. If I were given any maths classes in Trinity School, any staff who were passing our classroom commented, as the pupils and I joyfully shouted forth these songs, that it would have been better had I stayed in the relatively sound-proofed music room!

THE USE OF 'SECONDARY ROLE' IN PRIVATE TUTORING OF PUPILS IN ENGLISH LANGUAGE AND LITERATURE

Most of the private tutoring of pupils in the subjects of English language and literature that I was employed to do was by the means of what Dorothy Heathcote described in her mandate: "Sometimes you just need a road map." However, with the very young pupils who needed help with their written English, objects used in secondary role proved very useful.

Friends had given me very small hippopotamus objects made of ceramics, metal or plastic which normally perched on a shelf in my flat. However I pressed them into service in order to assist very young pupils, who, tired after a day's work at school, were required by their parents to have extra tuition in their failing written English. I thus enabled different tiny hippos to take different roles in the presentation of the subject. Some of them represented punctuation marks – full stops, commas, quotation marks, question marks etc and wherever one of these was appropriate in the work that the pupil was writing, I would make them pop up, and jump up and down, indicating that they should be used at that point. If the pupil did not use them correctly, I would make the hippos lie on their backs as if with disappointment and disapproval. There were other hippos who functioned as general critics of the work being written, being made to leap in the air if pleased, or lie on their backs with disapproval if disappointed with the work. By this means the pupils enjoyed the lesson as a game and gradually learnt the correct use of writing the English language by associating its components with their hippo equivalents.

I had found how attractive hippopotamuses were to the special needs pupils as teaching aids in secondary role and continued their use with young abled children. Consequently, friends who wondered at the number of imitation hippos in my flat were told: "Oh, they are all working hippos!"

Caution needs to be observed, however, in making sure that the pupil ultimately dissociates the object functioning in secondary role from what it represents. My mother, who was an infant teacher, spoke of her failure in this regard many decades ago. She was having a problem in making it clear in a spelling lesson to one of her pupils the function of the silent 'e' on the end of words such as 'make' and 'made'. It had been the custom in the school where she taught to make a saying of this which the children would enjoy reciting: "M-ade, made, with a lazy little 'e' on the end."

My mother decided to materialise the lazy little 'e' as a hen on an egg in order to make the concept of the 'e' at the end more real and she found a picture to illustrate this. However the device did not work as intended and the child did not dissociate the picture from the idea it represented, and simply adapted the saying into a new and more interesting form: "M-ade, made, with a lazy little hen on the egg."

Some of my mother's stories about her pupils reinforce Dorothy Heathcote's opinion of children's unique and intense understanding of the material world which needs to be addressed in their learning. This was one pupil's response to a composition on the subject she gave them of 'milk': "Mother's milk is best for baby. And the cat can't get at it."

I include these teacher's anecdotes from the 1920s in order to demonstrate the historic nature of Dorothy Heathcote's concerns and observations of education. She would often reinforce this point herself when she said, "Don't throw the baby out with the bath water," asserting that good teaching practices and mantras from the past should not be discarded.

She certainly maintained at least one ancient teaching ideal herself. When one of the actors who was participating in the *Antony and Cleopatra* workshop and also beginning a teaching career asked her what advice she could give him, she instructed him in another principle of teaching which she held dear: "Just love them."

In my early student days I had discovered the historic truth of that in a Latin text from ancient Rome: *Magister discipulos amat*. The teacher loves the pupils!

CHAPTER TEN

Conclusions

1 – Dorothy Heathcote's strategies which she incorporated in her drama-in-education programmes can create life-learning in any sphere, as in this study from: the technical world of mechanics, the business world of secretaries, the theatre world of drama students and professional actors, the music-appreciation world and the world of written English of young people. They can create learning for anyone in the community from young or older people learning a trade or profession through to disabled young people and adults.

2 – The use of analogy is successful as a means of leading students from the known to the unknown.

3 – Dorothy considered that the universals of the human condition should comprise the subject of school and college curricula. The plays of Shakespeare can provide many universal themes which can form the basis of exploring the world in terms of created scenarios. The themes of only three comedies were used in the experiments recorded herein, but the tragedies such as *Hamlet*, *Othello*, *Macbeth* and *King Lear* offer universal themes of such depth that profound life-learning could be experienced.

4 – Sometimes the work through drama-in-education on universal themes in Shakespeare's plays can lead not only to life-learning but to psychological release for the participant.

5 – Themes from plays written by Shakespeare can be applied to contemporary life.

6 – Sometimes ordinary people (like the Southgate Technical College motor vehicle mechanics) find the same solutions to problems within the themes from the plays and create the same stories from those themes as Shakespeare himself did.[1]

7 – Plays written by Shakespeare provide an excellent source of material for a variety of subjects in school and college curricula.

8 – The use of people in role in drama-in-education is of great benefit to the learning experience and classroom management of students.

9 – Girls of the same age as young boys in drama-in-education sessions are excellent in role, often relating more effectively to the students than older people.

10 – Drama-in-education can involve students, especially those suspicious of 'middle-class culture' in learning which they are often unprepared to explore in oral or written work.

11 – A television studio can provide an incentive for young people to make filmed dramas within which they may experience learning.

12 – The themes chosen for a class needed to be very strong in order to hold the respect of the class (see relative failure with MVM 1A in 1978–79 and at the Summerfield Centre in 2000–01 and the contrasting success with MVM 2D in 1979–80).

13 – Drama-in-education can demonstrate that students not considered to be creative or imaginative have inherent interpretive, imaginative and acting ability which they are willing to put into practice if given the opportunity. Presumably people from other occupations and ranks of society than the mechanics students of the above experiment would benefit should the opportunities be given to them.

NOTES

Preface

1 – Quoted from *The Guardian* obituary of Dorothy Heathcote on 17 November 2011.
2 – Georges Polti's *The Thirty-Six Dramatic Situations* was originally published in French in 1895; it was translated and published in English in (1916) New York: Scholars Choice; and more recently (11 November 2013) Charleston: Nabu Press. This book continues the work of Carlo Gozzi and is a descriptive list, categorising every dramatic situation that might occur in a story or performance.
3 – The company ran from 1976 to 2011 (see www.ts-u.co.uk) and then its venues and gear were transferred to The Festival Players (see www.thefestivalplayers.co.uk).
4 – In the years when these workshops were held, this Further Education College for those with special needs was known as Mencap National College, Dilston, owned and operated by Mencap. In 2014 it was sold to the Cambrian Group plc and renamed Cambrian Dilston College. For an illustrated item on the *Antony and Cleopatra* workshop see www.ts-u.co.uk.
5 – (1995) Portsmouth: Heinemann; (2016 reprinted 2017) Norwich: Singular Publishing.

Chapter One

1 – The scope and status of the college and its courses has now been widely expanded, combining with Barnet College as 'Barnet and Southgate College'.
2 – Objectives of this subject were: to increase knowledge, to foster understanding and to promote development through such topics as 'The media', 'Consumers' rights', 'The environment – use and misuse', 'Young motorists and the law', 'Money matters – personal and national', 'Holidays and recreational activities', 'The Universals'. (All courses for younger students included English and Liberal Studies, claiming that these would "prepare them for the day they become adult and ready to undertake their full responsibilities in the community". The aims and objectives included 'Alternative technology', 'Comparative religion' and 'Love, sex and marriage'.)
3 – pp.22–23 in Tim Taylor's book *A Beginner's Guide to Mantle of the Expert*.
4 – See additional books on Dorothy Heathcote: *Dorothy Heathcote on Education and Drama: Essential Writings* Edited by Cecily O'Neill (2014) London & New York: Routledge (for a comprehensive list of references, selected books and articles on Dorothy Heathcote and drama-in-education, see this publication); *Collected Writings on Education and Drama* by Dorothy Heathcote, edited by Liz Johnson and Cecily O'Neill (1984) London: Hutchinson; *Drama for Learning* by Dorothy Heathcote and Gavin Bolton (1995) Portsmouth:

Heinemann; *Heathcote at the National: Drama Teacher, Facilitator or Manipulator,* by Dorothy Heathcote (1982) Pembrokeshire: Kemble Press; *Exploring Theatre and Education* by Dorothy Heathcote (1980) Oxford: Pearson.

5 – The college employed a team of full-time technicians who serviced the departments with a comprehensive range of technical aids to their teaching. The small TV studio consisted of two rooms – one the control centre, soundproofed from the other curtained room where there were three cameras mounted on moveable stands and an overhead mirror (intended for showing for filmed cookery displays etc). There were two specialised technicians qualified to operate the TV studio – one the senior technical staff member. Usually one of these two assisted the students in our filming but if they were not available I was allowed to run the studio by myself if the class were competent and not disruptive.

6 – Accessed 07.09.2020.

7 – The exception to this was when the behaviour of class MVM 3 was so disruptive in the classroom that the TV studio was booked every week for them as it had a controlling effect on them.

8 – Acceptable to the motor vehicle apprentice students were *The Long, the Short and The Tall* by Willis Hall and *The Coming of Stork* and *Jugglers Three* by David Williamson.

Chapter Two

1 – There was a problem in the college regarding the status of drama as a course subject or its application to other courses. Some members of staff complained that the students spent too much time on their practical drama work to the detriment to their other studies. Certain members of staff of the Motor Vehicle Department regarded the subject as trifling, hinted at by the results of the field of drama being called 'plays'. These objected to my contacting the students at their workplaces in order to invite them to the Theatre Set-Up productions. This informal and personal approach to telephoning the students at work was the best way, I had discovered, of encouraging them to come to the performance. Fortunately there were other members of staff who were interested in the drama-in-education workshops and were supportive.

Chapter Three

1 – It was interesting to observe that perhaps some of the boys would have liked careers in fields other than that of motor vehicle maintenance.

2 – The departure of the girls was significant – as they realised that they were not really needed by the class in order to interest them in the drama-in-education work. In fact this class, in spite of their tiredness at the end of the day and week, were so involved with the drama and filming work that uniquely among all the mechanics classes, they were capable of working independently of the A level Drama students.

3 – In the years during which this work was done I never found any signs of racial prejudice in the College. Regardless of race, everyone behaved and was treated in the same way. There was integrated casting in the college productions and such was the equality of the students in all classes that the standards of work achieved were universally high.

Chapter Four

1 – The class became very creative in the setting and scenario of these episodes.

2 – As these students were older than the

other classes they were more concerned with the problems that they were experiencing in their own lives with regard to finding a wife, so I was pleased that they chose to explore the subject in their scenarios.

Chapter Five

1 – An example perhaps of life imitating art!
2 – The results achieved by this class alone would have validated the filmed drama-in-education work to any sceptics of the experiment.

Chapter Six

1 – The members of the management of the Summerfield Centre were pleased with the film work done with the students and to my surprise gave me copies of all the films.

Chapter Seven

1 – In p.31 of the chapter on 'Creativity', in *Dorothy Heathcote On Education and Drama,* O'Neill cites Dorothy reporting a similar opinion on the appropriate content of the teaching syllabus in a quotation by Sir Edward Hall that "Education should be related with transformation rather than information only". (From Hall. E. T. (1959) *The Silent Language*, London: Anchor Books.)

Chapter Eight

1 – Theatre Set-Up specialised in performing in heritage sites, mostly out of doors. The pleasure of enjoying the beauty of the site was part of the experience of the evening for the audience and often encouraged people who would normally not go to theatre events to attend – especially if picnicking was allowed! Sometimes people who on one occasion had attended the performance in order to assist with the transport and setting up of a picnic and the subsequent enjoyment of eating it during or before the performance, became drawn into liking the play and they subsequently continued to attend in future years. Theatre Set-Up always costumed the plays in well-executed period dress which enhanced the heritage backdrops (see the photo gallery, www.ts-u.co.uk).

2 – See *An Actor Prepares* (2013) London: Bloomsbury Academic (translated into English by Elizabeth Reynolds Hapgood and first published in Great Britain in 1937 by Geoffrey Bles).

Chapter Nine

1 – An example of what I considered to be the required application of inappropriate curriculum content to be studied by many special needs pupils was highlighted during an Ofsted inspection of the Trinity School. Much to the distress of the excellent teacher concerned, a complaint was made against her for not following the National Curriculum in a junior class of extremely disabled pupils. Typical of their disability was that of one of the pupils whose brain within her skull was only the size of a walnut. This pupil's dedicated school carer claimed that however much she used what little brain she had, she was not able to speak, write or follow the same curriculum as that studied by more abled pupils and that the Ofsted criticism was therefore not valid.

Chapter Ten

1 – See the ultimate of this principle in the student work in chapter 6 on *The Tempest*.

DR DOROTHY HEATHCOTE MBE, 1926–2011

Dorothy Heathcote was an innovator in the practice of drama-in-education as a means of promoting life-learning. Her 'Mantle of the Expert' strategies and techniques which continued to evolve over the years made learning possible for most subjects for any person, and her genius made it possible for her to work successfully within the full range of society, from disabled children and adults to inmates of prisons. Social equality was a hallmark of her work, demonstrating the innate creativity of all people, regardless of their education or social background.

Beginning her working life as a mill girl working three looms at the age of fourteen in her native Yorkshire, her innate talent was spotted and supported by a colleague who made it possible for her to become highly educated, trained in theatre and teaching and on the ultimate path to becoming the world-renowned lecturer in the Drama-in-Education and Master of Education courses of the University of Newcastle-upon-Tyne.

So popular were her methods of using drama as a means to realise learning that she was invited to many countries throughout the world to demonstrate her technique in workshops and lessons. Her worldwide popularity continued after her death and has recently created an increased interest throughout many countries in her vital use of drama-in-education to enhance life-learning. Films and books about her work keep this interest alive and make the rigour of her enlightened methods accessible to all. She was a trustee of Theatre Set-Up from 1996 until her death, seeing the plays every year, encouraging the actors performing in them and conducting several workshops.

DR WENDY JEAN MACPHEE (1938–)

Wendy was a teacher and lecturer in English, Drama and Music from 1960 to 2012 and was the founder of and a performer in the international professional Theatre Set-Up. She now writes books – see *Secret Meanings in Shakespeare Applied to Stage Performance* (2018), www.wjm-pyramid.uk and www.wjm-travelogue.net (2019) and *Upstaged by Peacocks* (2020)

www.ingramcontent.com/pod-product-compliance
Lightning Source LLC
Chambersburg PA
CBHW040416100526
44588CB00022B/2844